RICHARD ROAD
Journey from Hate

Return

FORTY YEARS AFTER LEAVING Germany, I was going back. I felt uncomfortable and I wasn't sure I was doing the right thing. I could imagine Mom looking at me, her hands firmly planted on her hips, unsmiling, shaking her head back and forth in disapproval.

"I don't believe it. You're not actually going back to Germany? After all they did to your family? Remember your cousins? Why, there are still SS Troopers they never caught. I've heard stories about..."

When I rented a car at the Frankfurt airport, a blonde woman quickly found my reservation and asked for my driver's license and passport. She was curt and business-like and looked bored with the whole process. As she wrote down my passport number, she suddenly stopped and looked at me carefully.

We had conversed in English and, for a moment I was overcome by a sense of fear. "You must be Jewish," I imagined her saying, "I'm sorry but..." To my surprise and relief, she smiled warmly. "You're a real German," she said. "You were born in Frankfurt. Welcome home."

International Standard Book Number:
0-87012-811-6

Library of Congress Catalog Card Number:
2011962262

Printed and published in the United States of America
by McClain Printing Company,
Parsons, West Virginia

Book design by Mary Wallis Gutmann
Body Type, Palatino

RICHARD ROAD
Journey from Hate

LUD GUTMANN

Table of Contents

Section One
Germany

Section Two
America

Continued on next page

Table of Contents

Continued from previous page

Section Three

School

Section Four

Wartime

Section Five

Dissonance and Harmony

Epilogue

The devotion of Rosi and Salomon to their sons
made everything possible

Germany

REGENSBURG, 1935

THE WARM SUMMER SUN sat low in the early evening sky, its rays reflecting brilliantly off the gothic spires of St. Peter's. The pale soft gray stone cathedral dominated the smaller buildings surrounding the Domplatz. The air was still clear as tiny bees buzzed around the red and white geraniums that overwhelmed the railing of the old outdoor restaurant.

It was the end of a long day for both my father, Sally (his given name was Salomon but no one ever called him that), and Ernst, Mom's older brother. They had been seeing customers in Regensburg and agreed to meet for dinner. Sally had given Gerhard, his chauffeur, the afternoon off. "The shops are all close by," Sally told him. "I can walk from one to the next. Besides, I need the exercise."

A smile spread across Gerhard's boyish face. "My wife will appreciate that."

"I'll ride back home with my brother-in-law after dinner and meet you early tomorrow morning," Sally said. He watched the Chrysler disappear around the nearby corner before beginning the first of his afternoon calls. His leather briefcase felt heavy, tugging on his shoulder, full of orders. He flexed his arm, lifting the overstuffed bag up to his hip. Good exercise, he thought.

Sally was a boxy-shaped man who always weighed twenty pounds more than he needed. His thick fringe of brown hair—he blamed wearing a steel helmet in the war for his early baldness—was neatly trimmed and partly covered by his gray fedora. He'd inherited his long aquiline nose from his father and had told my mother, Rosi, that he was glad I hadn't inherited his eagle's beak.

Sally walked the last few blocks to the restaurant lost in thoughts of the political turmoil surrounding his life. The sound of his leather heels, clicking lightly on the ancient cobble stones, reverberated from the nearby stone buildings. Sally, like Ernst, was a successful salesman. Ernst had introduced Sally to his sister, Rosi, and had been a major influence in arranging their marriage. Sally had just celebrated his fortieth birthday and, at this moment, his future looked uncertain. His life wasn't turning out as he had planned. He was anxious to talk with Ernst, to get his opinion on the state of things.

Sally was surprised that the Innenstadt—the city center—was deserted. Maybe it's a bit early, he thought. Ernst was already at the restaurant, sitting in the café garden.

It was early spring, but the planter boxes were filled with red and white geraniums and the waitresses with their white blouses and green skirts matched them for color. Ernst waved to be sure Sally saw him. Sally hung his suit jacket next to Ernst's on a hook carefully fitted into the stone wall behind their table. He sat down, undoing the bottom button of his vest. They were the only two people having dinner outdoors but still they kept their voices low like two conspirators plotting a devious plan. Two Jewish shoe salesmen in downtown Regensburg discussing the plight of Jews in Germany was a conversation best not overheard.

The waitress brought menus and they exchanged innocuous family news until after they had ordered and wine had been brought. "Regensburg is a nice city with a long Jewish history," Ernst began, "but they have not always been kind to the Jews. The city's history is rich with tales of fiscal extortion and confiscation of Jewish properties through generations. The Germans seem to be planning the same thing again, but maybe this time on a grander scale."

"The Nazis have taken over our country in three short years," Sally said. "It's not safe being Jewish. Jewish doctors can't work in hospitals anymore, Jewish professors have been forcibly retired or dismissed from the universities, and Jews in the government have been simply removed—so much for the Republic."

"Businessmen like you and me are still safe," Ernst replied. "The government needs us and our companies to keep the economy going but how much longer will it be before we are harassed and maybe," his voice dropped to a whisper, "maybe sent to concentration camps for the so-called re-education? Hitler has declared us the cause of all of Germany's problems and more and more people seem to believe him."

"It's not that we are the cause of anything," Sally said, looking grimly at Ernst, "It's that we are different—that we are not Christians."

Ernst shifted uncomfortably in his chair. "It was only fifteen years ago that we were in the trenches fighting a war for the Fatherland and now Hitler says we're not really Germans. It was fine to be Jewish and German and a soldier then when the Kaiser needed everyone to fight." Ernst gulped his Riesling.

"It's not just the Jews that Hitler is after. Others who

have spoken out, good people who have not agreed with his hysterical ranting have also been removed from the government and universities or worse, killed," Sally said. "We have had so much poverty since the war, the young unemployed people see Hitler as their great hope."

"And he is our greatest enemy," Ernst added, nodding his head.

"Rosi and I have begun talking about immigrating to the United States," Sally leaned forward, his voice a whisper, his wine forgotten. "Ludwig is already two years old and he can't have any future here."

"Getting to the United States is difficult," Ernst said. "You have to have an affidavit from someone who'll guarantee you won't cost the state any money if you can't get a job. Have you got someone who'll do that?"

"Rosi says Aunt Sarah in New York might be persuaded…" Sally looked up and his voice trailed off. He could see the young dark-haired waitress approaching. She placed a large plate filled with roast venison, dumplings, and cranberry sauce in front of him. They sat quietly until she left. The square was still strangely unpopulated, only a small flock of large, dark gray birds settled for a moment and then, following their leader, moved on.

Ernst waited for his sauerbraten to arrive. "Go ahead, start. I see her coming back with my dish," he said. After the waitress left, Ernst looked around to be sure they were still alone. "Yes, Sally, I agree, Aunt Sarah, my mother's sister, would be a good possibility for a sponsor. Her husband made a fortune as a wholesale butcher in New York. She always had a special liking for my little sister. She never approved of Papa putting Rosi in the orphanage when our mother died. Rosi was so little but Diena, Papa's new wife, was determined—she didn't want her at home. Friedel and I were okay as far as she was concerned since we were older and could help with the farm work."

Ernst paused, "How is my sister doing?"

"She's all right," Sally answered, "but every day there seems to be some incident that upsets her. She wants to leave Germany and is determined to write to her Aunt Sarah in New York to sponsor us but I'm not sure I want to go to America. She says she can't write until I make up my mind and we argue back and forth about it. She's obsessed about Ludwig—that he has no future here—and I know she is right."

"I'm as worried about my little Manfred and Ilse as you are about Ludwig," Ernst said, "but, you're right, America is a difficult choice. How can you be in business there and not speak English? We are both too old to become fluent in a new language easily. It will take years to be proficient. And we've worked so hard to get where we are—to be comfortable—after our early years being poor and growing in small farming villages. It's terrible to think of having to give up our careers and lose most of what we own. I'm going to try smuggling money and jewelry out of Germany. But now I've heard that Switzerland or France might be better choices than America, so I don't know..." Ernst took another swallow of wine. "If all else fails, I'd consider going to Palestine. It might be exciting to help build a Jewish state."

Sally knew that Ernst was a devoted Zionist and that Palestine had a strong attraction for him. For Sally, it came down to meeting his responsibilities to his wife and son—to save them from the tyranny of Germany—the idea that this might mean starting again, to establish a new career, was still beyond his thinking.

"I admire your nerve, Ernst," Sally said quietly. "I can't imagine life in another country, trying to do business in another language. I certainly don't have the courage to take the chance at smuggling. I don't know what happens if you're caught with money or gold. If we go,

WAISENHAUS

ROSI WAS ALONE. She sat, leaning forward on the big living room sofa, her hands firmly clenching her knees. Her breath came in angry gasps. Dried tears stained her cheeks. Rosi's tears were rare—something had happened. Luckily I was having a nap. A child of three might have objected to this man's rudeness toward his mama.

Just a few minutes before, she stood in the foyer while an imposing Gestapo officer scolded her for slapping her so-called Aryan maid. She had seen these black-suited men with their swastika armbands on the streets from afar but this young man was standing so close she could smell the stale cigarette smoke emanating from his clothes. He sneered at her. It took her breath away. He stood straight-backed in his crisply-tailored uniform and spoke in tones meant to intimidate.

His reprimand began as soon as Rosi identified herself. "Frau Gutmann," he said, looking down at her, "the mistreatment of your maid, a true German woman, is unacceptable. Physical abuse of a German is a crime against the state. I can assure you that this incident will be reported. Should this ever happen again, you and your husband will be arrested. You cannot get away with this behavior in the new Germany of 1936."

He nodded his head and placed his note pad in his jacket pocket. Turning around smartly on his polished black boot heels, he nodded to her and quickly left, slamming the door behind him.

I can picture Rosi in our spotless Dresden apartment. The thirties-style wood furniture, the cream walls and polished wood floors with good rugs, the rust and orange paisley upholstery colors setting off the tan skirt and white blouse she was wearing. The furnishings spoke of success and comfort.

Sitting on the sofa, the words still stung, "…you and your husband will be arrested." Rosi wanted to explain, to tell the officer that she'd never slapped the girl; she had scolded her for sunning herself instead of cleaning the apartment. A good German woman should have no problem working, she thought sarcastically. But I'm glad I didn't say anything back to him. No good could have come from trying to set him straight.

Rosi was a demanding woman. She expected a lot from herself as well as those around her, and she knew it. The maid was not being conscientious about work and that made her angry but it was the officer who infuriated her. This smug, self-important man warning her about prison for expecting an honest day's work from her maid was insufferable. He was more than pompous and arrogant—he was an intolerant anti-Semitic Nazi. If she weren't Jewish, the event would never have happened. The tears drying on her cheeks were those of frustration and anger. She had never met such a dangerous man.

Sitting motionless on the couch she was flooded by the same sense of helplessness she felt as a young girl the day her papa took her to the orphanage soon after her mother's death. She sat still, barely breathing, remembering that day and feeling the same fear of the unknown again after the Nazi's threat.

Memories of her mother flooded Rosi's mind. When she was six, it seemed that her mama cried almost all the time. Some days she would spend hours weeping in bed. Rosi would crawl in with her and Mama would hug and kiss her. After a while she and Rosi would go in the kitchen and Mama would get Rosi a glass of cold milk.

Years later, Brother Ernst told Rosi that the crying began after his twin sister, Martha, died of rheumatic fever. The doctor tried to help Mama overcome depression but nothing made her better. The whole family worried about her.

One day, Papa found her in bed, still, not moving and not breathing. The doctor rushed in with a helper and they took Mama to his house across the street. Rosi remembered watching silently as her Mother was carried away, knowing that something awful had happened but not sure just what.

Her brother, Friedl, sat down with Rosi in the barn room downstairs in the house—the room where the cows slept and where Papa got the milk. Sitting on a pile of hay, Friedl told her, "Mama's gone away," he was crying. Rosi hugged him and cried with him. "She's gone to take care of Martha," he said.

"When will she be home?" Rosi asked.

"She's not coming back," Friedl let out a giant sob. "We have to look after ourselves," he paused, "but I'll take care of you." He squeezed her hand.

Today's anger and fear were the same as her feelings long ago. In spite of her brother's best efforts he could not protect her—she was a little girl again, and all alone.

When Mama had been too sick and sorrowful to look after the family, a young woman named Diena would come to their house. She wasn't as pretty as Mama but she was a hard worker and Papa liked her. Rosi often stood in the backyard watching her vigorously scrubbing shirts and pants with brown soap on the metal washboard. She never spent much time with Rosi but she liked talking with Ernst and Friedl.

Soon after Mama died, Diena began to come every day. Before long, she moved in, sharing Papa's bedroom. The family room and kitchen were on the first floor next to the cow room. The three bedrooms were upstairs. They were all small but Papa had the biggest, the boys shared one, and Rosi had the smallest.

Before dinner one evening, Papa stood up at the head of the table and made an announcement. "Diena and I are getting married. She will be your new mother."

The boys stopped talking. The look on Ernst face said, no good can come of this. Friedl looked over at his little sister but neither boy said a word. They knew there was more to come.

Papa looked down at his plate. "Diena is going to have a baby so we'll need Rosi's room. It will be best if she went to the Waisenhaus."

The Waisenhaus. Friedl had told her about the Jewish orphanage for girls in the nearby town of Babenhausen and once on a trip to town she had seen the girls, walking together down the street, wearing blue uniforms underneath their white pinafores. Friedl said they were on their way to school.

Rosi began to cry. All she could think was, I don't want to wear the blue uniform, I want to stay home with Papa and my brothers, but she knew better than to speak. Friedl, sitting next to her, picked her up, holding her tight to his chest.

"So what happens to us?" Ernst asked. He was the oldest, tall and lanky, with dark eyes and brown curly hair. Rosi thought he looked the most like Mama. Friedl was shorter and heavier than Ernst. He looked a lot like Papa. Diena sat at the foot of the table. She was clearly in control. "You are big boys," she said. "You are both teen-agers. Your father needs you to help with the work and so do I." Looking at Rosi, she added, "Rosi is too little."

"Ernst and I can take care of her," Friedl said. Ernst nodded but Papa just shook his head, no. The boys knew it was Diena's decision, not Mayer's, and there would be no changing Diena's mind.

Babenhausen was too far away for Mayer and Rosi to walk. One of the neighbors lent his horse and wagon for the trip to the Waisenhaus. Her two brothers watched quietly, leaning against the thick grape vines growing up the side of the tan stone house. Mayer waited while she ran to them. She hugged them both and they bent over to kiss her. She kept looking back at them as she and her father began the ride to her new home.

The memory of that ride stayed with Rosi all her life. The sound of the horse's clopping hoofs on the cobble-stones, people stopping momentarily to watch them ride by, the feeling of being abandoned when her father waved goodbye after handing her little suitcase to the head-mistress—Rosi could recreate all of her feelings of dread.

She had thought the orphanage might be like a prison and she felt sick and afraid as she and her father rode there together. Maybe that was why she thought about it now—the specter of prison dangled by the Nazi officer brought back the unease of long ago. As it turned out, the women who ran the Waisenhaus were kind but strict. Obeying rules and being diligent and meticulous were lessons she learned growing up there.

Rosi missed the warmth of being home with her moth-er and brothers. Now she looked forward to her father's visits every month. He would always bring a favorite wurst and they would eat it together while they talked about home, but there was no mention of Rosi's return.

She told me many years later that I walked into the

living room, rubbing the sleep from my eyes, the day the Nazi officer visited her and aroused her from her reverie. She was glad I was taking a nap when he had given her his lecture. They, Rosi and Sally, had decided it was important to shield me from the political turmoil brewing all around us. She and I went downstairs so I could play in the sandbox while she waited for Dad to come home.

Sitting on a stone bench and watching me play, she thought, Sally will really be upset when he hears about my visitor. He hated confrontation and controversy and when it happened, he was always unhappy. He responded the same way to any reprimand. No, unhappy was the wrong word. Sally would be apprehensive and fearful. There were times when he could lose his temper, but his anger was always short-lived. The few times Rosi had been cross with him, he had cried. She had never seen a man cry—her brothers never did.

She knew it must have been the war. World War I had been a terrible experience for him and he would rarely talk about that period of his life. He had been wounded twice and was awarded the iron cross for bravery. And what was that worth, she thought bitterly? Sally had grown up in an orthodox religious home and battles and killing were anathema to him. Like so many other Jewish young men, he thought he had assimilated himself into German society but the current worsening anti-Semitism was redefining his status as a German.

When I was born, Dad wanted to name me Leopold after his father who had died three years earlier. Although it was the name of European kings, it had Jewish overtones. With Hitler newly coming into power—Paul von Hindenburg had named him Chancellor a few months earlier—Leopold was not a good idea. Six days before my birth, Jewish doctors, attorneys and shops were boycotted and, on my birthday, Jews were banned from holding population by the Nazi regime, his business had not been affected. The closing of stores owned by Jews had frightened him, however, and he knew Rosi was right when she insisted it would only get worse. Sally hated conflict. He solved most disagreements—if he couldn't charm his way out of them—by walking away. This time it wasn't as simple as leaving the room. This clash might change his life.

Sally had just been promoted to regional manager in Dresden and Willie Nathan and his two brothers, the owners of Ada-Ada, were delighted with the rapid increase in shoe sales. He had done so well on his Frankfurt route that they wanted him to duplicate his success in the Dresden area. So far, the Nazis had not taken any serious action against this Jewish shoe company and his customers, some of them Christian, were still buying Ada-Ada shoes. The thought that he might have to give it all up made him shudder.

Even though Sally was making progress professionally, German society was working against him. The Nazis were escalating their attacks on Jews. It was just a matter of time before they moved from shutting down small Jewish shops to taking over large Jewish-owned businesses. Ada-Ada would be a target.

As the car moved sedately through the gray early-morning streets, he looked out the window and considered his life. *I survived fighting in the German infantry years ago,* he thought, *but I'm not so sure I can survive this catastrophe.* Success was important to Sally. He had grown up in a small Bavarian town and his family was poor; his father had managed to eke out a living doing odd jobs for neighbors and selling an occasional cow or sheep. When Sally finished grade school, there hadn't been enough money to send him to the gymnasium for further schooling. His parents pleaded with his uncle to arrange an apprenticeship with Ladenburger and Wolf, a shoe and leather-goods manufacturing company in Karlsruhe, where he worked for four years until he was drafted into the German Army in World War I.

After his war years, he got the job with Ada-Ada and soon became their leading representative. His close friend from the leather-goods company, Eugene Neumetzger, told him, "Sally, you're a born salesman. You deserved that gold watch they gave you when you left for the war."

Sally knew emigrating from Germany would mean giving up everything he'd worked for and most of his savings as well, during a time of worldwide economic depression. He felt helplessly angry when he thought about it. If Hitler's anti-Semitic policies kept escalating, he was sure the owners would have to sell the factory at an undervalued price and he suspected they would leave Germany, too. He thought they might already be making plans.

He knew deep down that trying to escape with his family was inevitable but he felt indecisive about moving to America. Ernst was right, not knowing English was a major problem. Sally depended on his charm and skill with customers for his success as a salesman—not being able to converse would mean giving up his career. He feared having to struggle to support his family. But America was where Rosi wanted to go and Rosi was determined.

They had visited his sister Rosel the previous weekend. She and Julius, her husband, were convinced that Hitler's National Socialism would be short-lived.

Julius said firmly, "Anti-Semitism has always been a part of Germany's social fabric, we've lived with that, but the recent escalation, coupled with the removal of individual freedom and a return to an authoritarian form of government will prove to be intolerable to the German public. Loss of freedom will affect them too, you know."

months earlier that he had joined the SS. It was a casual remark said in passing. At first, Sally felt uneasy but Gerhard remained devoted to him and it was soon forgotten.

Gerhard continued, "I was looking through some files and was surprised to find one with the name of Salomon Gutmann. It contained a complaint about his wife slapping their maid. I managed to remove it and tear it up. She needs to learn to be more careful."

The car accelerated smoothly as Gerhard passed a van traveling slowly. He added, "I thought, my boss should leave our country with his family. It would be sad if anything happened to them."

Gerhard lapsed into silence. Sally opened his eyes. The green fields of wheat, barley, and sugar beets were a blur as Sally thought about what he had just heard. The danger was no longer theoretical. For a moment the old women in the field became three witches and their asparagus knives—bayonets. Watching the tall buildings of Leipzig loom on the horizon, Sally imagined them a huge prison built to torture the Jewish population. No, he thought, I have a long day's work ahead of me but, at the same time, I know I must take my family to safety—and quickly—no matter how hard it may be.

LEAVING

"JULIUS IS IN A CONCENTRATION CAMP," Rosi made the announcement in a breathless whisper as Sally came in the door carrying his leather briefcase bulging, as usual, with shoe orders. He had been on a several-day business trip.

She pulled Sally into the kitchen and shut the door. "The little one shouldn't hear this," she whispered, "he's already too nosy for his own good." Sally took off his jacket and laid it neatly on one of the kitchen chairs. "Listen," Rosi continued, "Julius got into an argument with a brownshirt who'd insulted him and was arrested."

"Who told you?" Sally asked.

"Who? Only your sister, his wife, Rosel, who else? She was there. She called me on our new telephone."

It wasn't so long ago that Rosi and Sally were excited about acquiring a telephone. Now, when its bell rang, Rosi was always in fear that it would bring bad news.

"She says he is in the camp for re-education," Rosi continued. " Re-education, you know what that means." Rosi was pacing up and down.

Sally shook his head and felt tears well up. Ernst had talked about the re-education imprisonments. No one ever talked about the experience when they got out and some never got out at all. He was sure they were all about torture and deprivation. It gave the government an excuse to take everything you had while you were locked up.

"I know what they mean by 're-education,'" he said. "I can't believe Julius would be fool enough to get into a dispute with the Nazis—but then, again, he has a hot temper. How's my sister handling it?"

"Rosel is so upset. She says she can't stop crying," Rosi said. "It's not a surprise that it happened. You're right. Julius has always been impulsive and gets infuriated too easily. Even if the brown shirts started it—and I'm sure they did—he should have backed down. What can we do for them? Nothing, probably, am I right?"

Sally nodded. "This time his anger got him into serious trouble," he said. "And you are right, we can't do anything for them; we're close to leaving." Sally's unspoken addition might have been, "We can't let anything jeopardize our escape."

Despite all the endless bureaucratic hurdles it did seem that we were leaving. Sally had been filling out forms for nearly a year. Sometimes it appeared close and other times there seemed no chance, but, finally, they had filled out the last form and had it approved with a Nazi swastika printed in the corner as a seal of authenticity.

After lengthy and mindless encounters with the government agents and threats of the new "flight tax"—a tax that could mean giving up many belongings and all property, the final permission to leave was granted. The all-important affidavit had been arranged with Aunt Sarah which made entry into America possible.

Tens of thousands of German and Austrian Jews would not be so fortunate.

Rosi and Sally had really wanted to go to Switzerland. Rosi's best friend, Bertel Unger, and her husband, Fritz, lived in Zurich. In Switzerland, language would not be a problem but Fritz had written that immigrating there was impossible. The country had closed its borders to Jews wanting to escape from Germany. Rosi believed Bertel and Fritz. Bertel had been one of her closest friends during her years in the Waisenhaus orphanage. As girls, they had always confided in each other and still did. Fritz was an attorney and they trusted his advice.

Sally sat on his favorite sofa chair after dinner thinking that Julius and his disaster were not the only fearful events. Lightning was striking all around them. The week before, he was leaving a major retail store where he had finished taking a large order from one of his best customers. The owner had so far, miraculously, escaped the Nazi's disenfranchisement of Jewish shopkeepers. Gerhard held the door of the Chrysler open.

As Sally dropped his stuffed briefcase on the floor and sat down, tired after a long day, Gerhard leaned in the car door and said quietly, "Before we go to the hotel, I wanted you to know that the owner of this store is being arrested tonight. I know you like him."

Sally dropped his hat on the floor next to the briefcase. Gerhard shut the door and moved to the front of the car. As he positioned himself in the driver's seat, he added quietly, barely moving his mouth and looking up into the rear view mirror, "We know he's been smuggling large amounts of money and jewelry to Switzerland. He will be sent to one of the camps."

Sally paused for a long moment. "I think I forgot my hat in his shop. I need to go back. I'll only be a minute."

When he returned Sally said, "My hat wasn't there. It was lying here on the floor of the car the whole time."

Gerhard just smiled.

Sally called the store the following morning. The woman answering the phone said her boss had left for Switzerland unexpectedly the evening before. He relaxed, but only slightly after barely sleeping the night before, worrying about his friend. It could have been me and my family, he thought; like lightning striking and missing by moments.

Sally and his brother-in-law, Ernst, had continued their conversation about getting money and jewelry out of the country every time they met. Ernst was a strong proponent but Sally did not share his aggressiveness. Sally was frightened he might be caught and incur the ire of the Gestapo. The idea of being arrested and sent to a camp horrified him—just seeing the uniformed gangsters on the street made him cringe. The episode with Gerhard reaffirmed his decision not to get involved with smuggling. It wasn't just fear of the camps, he knew if he was arrested Rosi and Ludwig would be helpless without him.

As a part of the permission that he and Rosi had obtained in order to leave Germany, the Nazis said they could take all their belongings but only a quarter of their savings with them. Hitler was continuing the process of stripping the Jews of their money but purchases of goods were all right—anything to stimulate the economy during the Great Depression. That stirred Rosi's rage.

"They are a bunch of hoodlums. I hate them," she said.

Sally was his business self and saw an opportunity. He sent Rosi out on a shopping spree. "Just buy whatever you think we might need in America. We'll put it all together with the furniture and household things in our shipping container."

"I'll start at Hertie," Rosie said. Hertie was Germany's best chain of department stores. "The Nazis may run it now, but at least it used to have a Jewish owner."

"And when we get ready to arrange our trip to America, we'll book passage on the best ship we can," Sally added. He was glad she had seen the wisdom of his plan. "Let's spend the money so the Nazi's won't get it."

Rosi bought Rosenthal china and fine cut glass, handsome Middle Eastern rugs, expensive sheets and towels, fashionable dresses and blouses, children's clothes, a new heavily-carved wood dining room set, and a luxurious Persian lamb fur coat. Making the purchases briefly calmed her constant anger toward the Germans—it was a moment of revenge—even if only short-lived. Of course, the profits went to the government, so the Nazis came out ahead, but Rosi was able to take some possessions.

The most serious uncertainties for Rosi had to do with relatives and friends. Some were ready to leave, others held stubbornly to the idea that the Nazis were a passing evil and would soon be rejected by the German public. She listed them in order of closeness in her mind.

Her biggest worry was Julius and Rosel and their three girls. They were in the most danger of all. There were two questions: would the Nazis release him and would the experience change Julius' mind about leaving? Her brother, Friedl, finally had decided to immigrate to America. Aunt Sarah promised to endorse an affidavit for him and his family. Rosi's other close Waisenhaus friend, Gertrude, had no family in America, so she and her husband were looking to South America.

Finally Rosi's brother, Ernst, had turned into a passionate Zionist and was beginning to talk about going to the Holy Land. Rosi wasn't surprised that he might go to Palestine. He had assimilated himself into German society but he had never lost his commitment to Judaism. The two didn't seem related in his mind; as a loyal citizen, he served in the army in the war.

Like Sally, he'd fought for the fatherland—the evil fatherland now, she thought, sarcastically—against the Russians in the east during World War I and later against the English, the French, and the Americans in the west.

So much for fighting for Germany, Rosi thought. These

men had risked their lives. Sally had almost been killed many times. Once, while lying in a shallow trench with his comrades, the noise of the machine gun next to him making a deafening noise, Sally moved away to try to find a less noisy place, taking cover in the nearby trees. Suddenly, there was a deafening explosion. When the smoke and dust had cleared, Sally stared for a moment in disbelief. All his comrades were dead. Sally felt pain in his scalp and warm blood running down the side of his neck. He pressed his handkerchief against the wound and moved deeper into the forest.

Rosi could feel anger rising inside. We are all being forced to leave this so-called fatherland, she thought, with everyone going in different directions, to unknown places. Who knows if the new countries are safe? She had heard about anti-Semitism in America and a pro-Nazi organization, the German American Bund, in New York— and that worried her. It didn't matter, they had to leave Germany and at least for now, America seemed a safe haven.

Rosi couldn't help worrying about all the relatives even though there was little she could do. Some were ready to leave, others had already gone, still others—often the older ones—couldn't be convinced to flee before it was too late. They didn't see the dangers or were just as fright- ened of the uncertainties that awaited them in a new country. She and her family were part of a new Diaspora. She tried to console herself with the thought that Diaspora was the fate of the Jewish people.

There was also Mayer, Rosi's father—Opa. He wasn't sure he wanted to leave his home in Schlierbach. Like many others, he couldn't make up his mind. Her step- mother had died which would make it simpler for Opa to emigrate. Rosi knew that once Ernst made his decision, he would push Opa hard to leave.

Sally's father had died a few years earlier and was spared the tragedies that were being imposed on the Jews at an ever-increasing pace. But there was Sally's mother, my Oma, who refused to consider leaving Germany. She was going to stay, no matter what. "This has been my home all my life," Oma said. "Besides, my daughter, Rosel, needs me to help her with the girls." Rosi knew there was no convincing her if Rosel wouldn't leave. Oma was getting old and forgetful and she was no longer making wise decisions.

Sally had told Rosi, "Ben might still convince her to leave and he could arrange it. She won't listen to me."

Ben was Oma's youngest and they had always had a close relationship. She had visited Ben a few years before in New York City where he lived but came back saying it was a strange country. "Everyone is running from one place to the next. Trains run over your head, there's noise everywhere, and I can't understand anybody."

Ben had lived in New York since 1927 and from gossip Rosi had heard, she never fully trusted him. Sally had to arrange for his brother to emigrate from Germany long before the Nazis came to power. The circumstances were never quite clear. Sally would never talk about it. There had been some fraud, she had no idea what Ben had done but guessed that it involved embezzlement, and he had left for America before she met Sally. The brothers were never close—Sally had always been the disapproving older brother but she knew Ben admired Sally and had invited them to stay with him and his family when they all got to New York.

If we get to New York, she thought.

THE NORMANDIE 1937

WHEN I WAS FOUR, we were ready to leave Germany. I knew we were going somewhere but it didn't mean much to me at that age. I have only scattered memories of the run-up to the trip while around me threats were growing that were emotionally charged and frightening to my parents.

One day I heard the apartment door shut quietly and guessed it was Papa coming home. He came over to my play table. "Have you been a good boy?" he asked, running his hand through my hair. "Did you help Mama with your little brother?" My father towered over me. He seemed huge as he leaned over me.

"Yes, Papa."

Papa put his briefcase down next to the sofa and took off his striped gray suit jacket. Still carrying it, he headed for the open bedroom door and peeped in.

"Nice to see that Franz is sleeping," Papa said. "It seemed like he cried all night."

"He's been good today," I heard Mama say. "Thank goodness he's only a baby so he can't talk and make problems. I wish Ludwig had been as good today."

"What happened?" Papa asked. I stopped and listened to the conversation; my four-year-old ears were sharp.

"Nosy," my mother always called me, "Nosy gets you into trouble." She paused, glancing at me, her face shrouded with concern. "Ludwig spent a lot of time playing outside—at first, in the sandbox," Mama said. "He was filling up his pail with sand and making cakes. I had him stop when he called to a nice grandmother, 'Heil Hitler, want to buy one of my cakes?' If he hadn't been so cute about it, I'd have really been upset."

"It's still disturbing," Papa said quietly, looking back at me, "even though he doesn't understand."

"Children just repeat what they hear other people say," Mama said. "Children imitate everything."

"Ludwig has an excuse," Papa replied. "He's just an innocent boy. Adults should recognize the malevolence of the Nazis but, instead, they all accept Hitler as their leader and salute him."

Mama paused. "Later we almost had a disaster," she continued. "He and his two friends were chasing each other and making a lot of noise."

"I can just guess what happened," Papa said. "That old Prussian in the villa next door..."

"Yes," Mama interrupted, "he was outside, hidden behind his huge hedge. Who knows what he was doing, probably trying to read a book."

"Or, more likely, trying to take a nap," Papa said.

"He kept yelling at the boys to be quiet," Mama said, "but you know how our son is. That old Junker threatened to call the police. That's just what we need now that we have permission to leave. Anyway, I finally had to bring him upstairs. Franz slept through the whole thing."

"That old Nazi could make trouble for us," Papa said. "I just want to get out of here without any problems." Then, as an afterthought, he added, "There are rumors that the Nazis are going to open a new concentration camp near Weimar.

The rest remained unspoken. Every year with Hitler as Chancellor had been worse than the one before: Jews were pushed to emigrate, doctors could not practice, the Swiss closed their borders to us, students were denied university degrees, and now a systematic takeover of Jewish properties was beginning. Rumors were becoming realities.

Rosi had survived her confrontation with the Gestapo officer only a few months before. Another similar episode and their plans could be devastated. The Junker was just another old man to me. I had no idea that we were about to leave our comfortable apartment for good and that a word casually spoken could jeopardize our escape. And as a four-year-old, I probably wouldn't have cared if I had known.

My next brief memory was of a brochure about the steamship, *Normandie*. My mother was watching me from across the living room as I sat on my chamber pot. It was gleaming white with a brown wooden ring-shaped seat on the top. Why do certain details remain in my recollections? I was squatting there, entranced, as I looked through a color pamphlet publicizing the new luxurious French ocean liner; an extravagant Art Deco design. The prospect of sailing on this magnificent ship filled me with excitement.

Mama played it up, "It's a new and wonderful ship, look at the three big smoke stacks. There's only one other with three and that's the *Queen Mary*. It's a spectacular ship—the best in the world—and we're lucky to be able to go to America on it in a first-class cabin so we'll be very comfortable." She didn't sound sad to be leaving; if there was any regret in her voice it didn't come across to me.

The three big smoke stacks dominated the picture of the ship. Billowing clouds of white smoke, streaked with black, rose up above them as the ship sailed on a smooth calm sea. But what really caught my attention was the picture inside of a puppet theater in the children's play-room. I saw that brochure more than sixty years later in the collection of the Museum of the City of New York. The beautifully-rendered pictures were exciting and as fresh as when I was a child. It took my breath away to see it again, just as I remembered.

"Will I get to see the puppets, Mama?"

"Of course, we'll watch the theater every afternoon. It'll be so much fun." She smiled at me. "And wait till you see the children's dining room," she continued. "The walls are covered with pictures of Babar the Elephant." I hadn't heard of Babar—he wasn't in Mom's repertoire of German stories—but those elephants were exciting.

Threats of war and attacks were striking in neighboring countries as we began our flight. My parents had finally pulled it together—the visas and the sponsorship and the lists of belongings and payments to transport companies were made just in time. After spending many hours at the various self-serving agencies of the newly-powerful government, in September 1937, our official passports were finally issued. They bore the Nazi eagle.

Four years later, on November 25, 1941, our family lost our German citizenships in absentia when a new law was issued, named: "11th Decree to the Law on Citizenship of the Reich," which stripped citizenship from all German Jews living outside of Germany. We were stateless from 1941 until my mother and father both became United States citizens and, therefore, we children as well. But, on the 1937 trip, we were still German citizens, emigrating to the United States.

At four years of age, I saw the train trip from Dresden to the French coast, the big modern cruise ship (a boat to me), the puppets and the elephants, as all one great adventure. I had no inkling of the horror that had prompted the trip. I didn't know that it was really an escape from an oppressive regime, not a vacation. I didn't know that Dad was giving up his career in order to evade possible death, and to find safety for all of us in a new country. Or that we all might, at the last minute, be denied passage and possibly be interned in a labor camp. Or that my mother and father had no clue as to what they might face in their new world. Or that my parents were worried about taking a baby, my little brother, on this long voyage. And I didn't imagine that we were never going home. To me, it was just an exciting journey.

I did know the things that were important to me: we were taking my new big lacquered metal bed, my favorite books, and all my toys. They were deep in the inside of the ship, in the hold; kept safe in a huge container.

I'm sure I must have told my mother she didn't have to take the book of Grimm's fairy tales. She would have smiled at this. She knew how scared I was of the first picture—the ferocious looking wolf, lying in Grandma's four-poster bed, Grandma's white cap on his head, hungrily eyeing little Red Riding Hood and her basket of goodies. But the book came along to terrify me in the United States. My mother saw it as merely a collection of traditional children's stories, nothing to fear—I wonder she never equated the wolf with Hitler. If she had, it might have stayed in Germany and not made the escape with us.

Dreams of seeing the puppet play, eating in the elephant-covered dining room, and running around the deck were shattered by the stormy weather and seasickness. There was no sunshine that September at sea—only wind, rain, and gigantic swells that rocked the great ship. I spent the whole trip sick in bed with Mom tending to my misery. The constant to and fro movement was soothing to the baby. Franz slept happily most of the time in his straw-colored wicker laundry basket. He has always been a good sailor.

Our visas had been carefully checked before leaving Le Havre. They would be examined again before we entered the United States.

When they were filling out papers for the United States customs, Dad reminded Mom, "Ben wrote that we need to pay close attention to how they spell our names. They often make mistakes."

"Maybe this is an opportunity to change the boys' names," Mom said. "We gave them traditional German names so they would fit in there. Now they might be better off with more American-sounding names."

"Franz is easy," Dad said. "He can be Frank. Ludwig is harder. We already decided against Leopold. We'd have to totally change his name."

Mom thought for a moment. "You're right," she answered. "Besides, for me he'll always be Ludwig." Since there was no easy change, there would be no change.

I missed seeing New York City slowly rise from the ocean, the grandeur of the Statue of Liberty, the multitude of smaller ships and our majestic French liner's slow entry into New York Harbor. I do remember the strange people who met us at the dock—everyone hugging one another.

"Where are my books and toys?" I asked, looking up at Mom.

"They'll be here soon," she said. She held my baby brother to her chest with one arm and tightly clasped my hand with her other hand. "We're staying with Uncle Ben and Aunt Clara here." They were two of the strangers who spoke a strange language mixed with a smattering of German. "They live in the Bronx and have a nice bed for you."

We were beyond reach of Hitler's fanatic regime—the regime that, ominously, predicted its survival for one thousand years. To me, it was an adventure with things to interest and excite a four-year-old. My parents had kept all their fears of danger brewing to themselves during my whole short life. We were safe but we were strangers in a foreign country that was in the middle of an economic depression as severe as the one in Germany. The trip on the *Normandie* was the last taste of luxury my parents knew. This was the beginning of the most difficult and challenging period for my parents—and I had no idea.

SECTION TWO

America

A New Beginning

"PICK UP YOUR FEET," the old woman demanded, "and take off your hat." I looked up and all I could see were her intense brown eyes boring into me. I reached up for the security of my mother's hand but it was plucking the beret off the top of my head.

"Listen to the teacher," Mom said firmly, "she's right."

It was my first visit to the neighborhood school and it seemed a replay of my first day in Washington Heights not long after we moved in. There, down on the sidewalk, I received my introduction to English, "ged adda heah."

Welcome to America. I only remember the words, not the looks of the kid who said them, but the sentiment was widespread.

In New York City we were part of swarms of people of many nationalities and dozens of countries who were arriving daily. But we German Jews were a bit different. We were Germany's outcasts while Hitler's plans for world domination were falling into place.

In 1937, the formal declaration of the beginning of World War II was a few years away but the horrors inside Germany and in other European countries because of Germany were growing. Unlike many other depression-era immigrants who had left a life of poverty, hoping for a better life—we fled our comfortable, middle-class society to save ourselves from death. Upper Manhattan was a teeming beehive of German Jews, desperate and determined to make a new beginning. We could not go back; we could only go forward.

Our family moved into a two-bedroom apartment on the fourth floor of an old tenement building with an elevator that didn't work most of the time. The graying paint was peeling off the walls and the elevated train—we discovered it was called the El—clattered deafeningly at all hours past the bedroom windows, waking us at night. When the trains rushed by, the red neon sign of the all-night grocery store across the street seemed to flash in a rapid fire on and off as its intense color was blocked every split second by the train. It was frightening at first and then just annoying.

The furniture that my mother brought from Germany looked strange squeezed into the decrepit surroundings. She moaned about the film of oily dust that came in through the open windows every day in summer and she spent hours cleaning and polishing, trying to keep the grime from destroying the luster.

Relatives were always visiting at our apartment, full of helpful advice on how to survive. Uncle Karl, Mom's younger half-brother, was a guard in a downtown factory. Uncle Ben worked as a bookkeeper in a manufacturing plant in Jersey City and sold life insurance in the evenings, and Dad's cousin, Uncle Felix, together with his wife, had developed a small company that made real raspberry syrup—only fresh fruit and no artificial coloring. This delicacy was highly prized by my mother who used it to cover the metallic taste of the tap water.

Dad quickly learned that there were no jobs for business executives who didn't speak English. He had known that would be a major problem before leaving Germany but now, for the first time, it hit home. Attempts to find menial work were equally unsuccessful.

"If you don't know English, there are no jobs," he said, sniffing back tears. "I don't know what I'll do."

Rosi was worried and not just because he couldn't get work to support the family. She had seen it twice before in their ten years of marriage. When Sally had reverses or problems at work he became disheartened and depressed and his depression was disabling. Twice in Germany he had spent a month in a sanatorium when there had been too many stressful events in his business life.

Sally thrived on hard work and success and literally withered in the face of adversity. Tears came and Rosi could see that his initial eagerness and anticipation after landing in New York were quickly sapped and he was overcome by a sense of hopelessness and despair.

Rosi thought, it's easier for me than it is for Sally. For me, it is all about my family. I gave up our comfortable life but not a business career. I can do what I do anywhere but, for him, he's in his forties—he should be reaching the peak of his profession. Instead, he's lost it all and has to start again, as if he's a young man. It's really hard for him.

We had been in New York for three months and for the last four weeks Sally had not left the apartment. He spent the days sitting in his overstuffed sofa chair staring at the ceiling.

"Why is Papa crying all the time?" I asked. "What's wrong, did he get hurt?"

"No, he isn't hurt," Mom answered. "At least, not in the way you would understand. Papa will get better. Go play with your toys and I'll read you a story later."

She watched me go over to my toy table in the living

his chair without taking off his jacket. "I quit work at the cafeteria today," he said, tears welling up. "There was a man who ate a big lunch and then refused to pay for his meal. He looked so poor, I felt sorry for him. Still, I told him he had to pay. He yelled at me—said that he would kill me when I finished work. I think he was serious. I'm not going back."

For a few months Dad tried selling life insurance. When he did business in German he was charming and charismatic, but it was difficult for him to carry it off even with his improving English. He was no longer the effective salesman he'd been and he was selling a less-needed product.

"I have to find something different to support us," he told Rosi. "We have gone through half of our savings. I must have a new line of work but I don't know where to begin. Maybe I need to get a good factory job like Ben—if I can find one. They don't seem to like immigrants except for the most menial work."

Over two years had passed since we'd arrived and Dad sat in his favorite easy chair reading the weekly German Jewish newspaper, *Aufbau*. It was a sweltering day in early June and Dad had on a pair of his old suit pants and a sleeveless undershirt, tiny drops of sweat clinging to his bald forehead. Mom sat at the kitchen table in a simple house dress and tan cotton stockings carefully darning one of Dad's woolen socks, a life-sized wooden egg stuffed into the heel, so it would keep its shape. My baby brother, Frank, slept in his crib and I was playing with some blocks on the other side of the table.

Mama looked over at Papa. "Why are you crying? Is it something in the paper?" she asked.

He looked up from the newspaper. "Our youngest son will be two years old soon and what is there to commemorate his birthday? Hitler destroyed hundreds of synagogues and thousands of Jewish businesses were ransacked last fall. And now they are sending thousands of Jews to concentration camps. The American people don't believe such a thing can happen."

Mama let the wooden egg fall to the floor as she got up from her chair to look at the paper over Dad's shoulder. "Damned Germans," she muttered, "and Rosel, Julius, their girls, and your mother are still trapped. There's nothing but bad news here and worse news from over there." I scrabbled under the table to retrieve the egg.

Uncle Ben, my father's younger brother, knocked on the door. Ben was full of charm and always had time for me. He had become my favorite relative and not just because he always had a present—today it was a white pencil with Prudential printed on its side—but also because he was usually positive about most things.

Ben was an energetic bantam of a man, who spoke English with only the slightest German accent, unlike my parents whose English was rudimentary. Of course, he had emigrated in 1927, so he'd had years of practice and, besides, he was much younger. Ben always said New York was the place he had chosen to seek his fortune. This day he had come to help Dad make a better transition to America. Ben never wasted time. He could see from the hastily-dried tears that something had been happening so he opened with a general statement to get the floor.

"This Kristallnacht business and now killing Jews in concentration camps is a disaster in the old country," he said.

Mom cut him off, "Sally's out of work again, and he hasn't done well selling insurance, but we are lucky to be here," my mother said quickly with no spaces between the thoughts, and as usual, talking about my father—talking about him, with him sitting there listening. Dad just looked up and waited. He knew there was a purpose for

Ben's visit. He hadn't come to discuss the events taking place in Germany.

"Have you heard about all those chicken farms for sale in New Jersey?" Ben asked. Dad nodded his head. "They say it's a new industry. If we go to war, eggs will be a major foodstuff. Lots of German Jews are buying farms."

"We know all that," Mom said. "There've been several articles in the *Aufbau*." Later we found that "lots" in Ben's vernacular was stretching the statistics.

"Well," Ben continued, "I know this man, Herman Kafka. He lives in Farmingdale, that's in New Jersey, and says he knows of a chicken farm for sale there. Maybe you should look into it."

"How far is it from New York?" Mom asked.

"Not so far," Ben replied. "Kafka says there's a bus from the city that goes there."

"Sally, it might be a good idea," Mom said, turning to Dad. I stopped playing and put my blocks back into their brown shoebox. I quickly stood up and stayed motionless, listening intently, my chin now resting on the kitchen table. I was always snooping and the recent changes in our lives had made me more curious than ever.

"I'm not sure we can afford it," Dad said.

"Mr. Kafka says the owner is charging ten thousand dollars," Ben responded.

"That's most of the money we have left. We've already spent half the savings we brought with us," Dad seemed uncertain. He looked at Mom and she nodded her head.

"We should look into it," Mom said. "We'll have to work hard but we can do it. Living in New York City is no good, there's nothing here for us. A farm would be good for the boys. It'll be a new beginning."

A new beginning—getting out of Germany and landing in New York had meant a whole new way of life for my parents—this would be a second new beginning.

The old ways in Germany of frequent visits to the theater, concerts, and the opera, summer vacations in the Black Forest and winter holidays in the Swiss Alps were now forgotten. A high-paying job with a large corporation, a big car driven by a chauffeur, a modern apartment with a maid—they were all part of a world destroyed by the Nazis.

Like the name of the German Jewish newspaper, America was all about *Aufbau*—rebuilding. But for us so far in New York, it was mostly about adjusting and surviving. The real *Aufbau* would begin on a farm in the middle of New Jersey.

THE FARM

NEW YORK CITY was a two-year prelude. Our life in America really began on the farm on Richard Road in Farmingdale, New Jersey.

After our New York apartment, the farmhouse seemed gigantic. It was two stories high, covered with white stucco and topped with a black shingle roof. A large wood front porch painted an earthy brown had a crawl space that immediately became my favorite hiding place—a six-year-old boy's dream.

The concrete back porch had a slanted white trap door set into one side that led down concrete steps to a cavernous basement. An acrid oily smell arose from a bin built into a corner half filled with coal. A bulky furnace, pipes spreading in every direction, dominated the dark entrance. It was here in the cellar that eggs were cleaned, weighed, and packed.

The farmhouse had three important rooms downstairs: a comfortable country kitchen, a parlor that was entered only with very clean hands, and a formal dining room that held a large table and chairs and a buffet for my mother's precious crystal and the Rosenthal china. This quiet place would turn out to be perfect for little brother Frank's daily music practice sessions.

The parlor, with a prominent sandstone fireplace, was sacrosanct. It housed all of my mother's treasured classics—books in German and recordings of music—in a built-in floor-to-ceiling bookcase that covered one wall. It came with the house. The room was used only for special occasions: entertaining company, listening to European operas and symphonies, and as a quiet place for my father's afternoon naps. My mother's heavy carved wood furniture from Germany found a comfortable home in New Jersey.

A bathroom and a small bedroom were in a corner of the first floor, behind the living room. The bedroom was called Opa's room. It was where grandfather slept on his visits once he arrived in America. To everyone's relief, he had finally been convinced to come. The rest of the time the room held laundry and linens and, because the room was always cold when Opa wasn't there, it also had the spicy aroma of the sausages that Mom would hang on a long rope stretched across the room to dry evenly.

The second floor had four large bedrooms and a second bathroom. Frank and I each had our own room. A third bedroom, the guest room, was always closed and of little interest. The largest bedroom was Mom and Dad's. It was packed full with two large beds that fitted together, two night stands, and two huge wardrobes, all finished in a rich dark mahogany veneer—more treasures from Germany. I liked sneaking into their bedroom to play with the drawers in the wardrobes which slid smoothly in and out and were filled with clothes and fine linen tablecloths and napkins.

There was one more room upstairs, and it became the *Koffer Raum*—or trunk room—and held my parents' many suitcases and steamer trunks, ready for the next move if the need arose. My mother was always ready. It was also where Mom kept the wicker clothes basket that had carried my brother across the Atlantic Ocean as an infant.

But best in the house was the large, airy kitchen. It had two windows and a door that looked out to the backyard, a stove, refrigerator, and a play table that held, besides toys, the sacred radio that brought the world in. I can see and hear our family gathered in this comfortable room, sitting at the heavy round wood table together. At this table we ate most meals, Dad and Mom conducted farm business, Frank and I did our homework, and we all listened to the radio.

The kitchen table was also the place where I sat under Mom's watchful gaze listening to the weekly Saturday afternoon Metropolitan Opera broadcasts with Milton Cross narrating. The never-ending arias of love betrayed, duets professing undying devotion, and the oratorios of the dying hero failed to compete with the images of the Lone Ranger riding across the western plains to the strains of the William Tell overture.

Every evening Dad would lift up his hand, signaling silence, as CBS radio's distinctive and controversial news commentator, Gabriel Heatter, began his broadcast. Everyone waited to hear if he would again begin with, "Ahhh, my friends, there's good news tonight, ladies and gentlemen, there's good news tonight"—and he always did. If the war news was bad, he reported it, but the good news was always first.

We were breathless when, in September 1939, we heard the radio announcement that Germany was at war with England and most of Europe. It came through the air across the ocean reported by BBC news with the crackling of electrical background interference that made it even more exciting and frightening. To me the war was fought by those intermittent voices that faded in and out and sounded so far away.

I don't think being Jewish had been important to Mom

and Dad when they lived in Germany—at least, not until Hitler made it a central issue. I don't believe they observed most of the Jewish traditions then, even though Dad's parents were Orthodox Jews. Mom and Dad considered themselves German and were steeped in German culture. Unlike the eastern European countries, the Jewish ghettos in the small towns and big cities of Germany had mostly disappeared. The German Jews had assimilated into German society. Or they thought they had.

Hitler's rise to chancellor in 1933 changed all that. There were many new laws, but on April 7, the day I was born, a decree was issued by the German Nazi government that removed (or retired) all Jews from public offices, and, finally, from academic life, from hospitals and clinics, and from the judiciary. World War I veterans, like my father and Mom's two brothers, Ernst and Friedl, who had fought on the German side, were supposedly exempt, but everyone was aware of the tightening noose. For a while, some Jews working in the private sector in business and finance were spared but my father could see the takeover in the making. Only because my father arranged for us to leave in 1937 were we able to escape with some of our worldly goods. But that all ended in 1938 with Kristallnacht.

Once Dad agreed with Mom that we must leave Germany, he began to take the necessary measures: getting government permission, planning what we could take along, and taking other necessary steps. Mom, for her part in the practical planning, wrote to Aunt Sarah for sponsorship. But she made another appeal which, to her, was as important—she made a covenant with God.

Mom meant it when she promised that she would embrace all the Jewish traditions and observe and obey the complicated rules and laws of Orthodox Judaism if she could get her family out safely. She took her side of her pact with God seriously. There would be no variations, no deviations, and no exceptions for anyone in the family for any reason—at least, in the beginning, when Frank and I were young. Being Jewish in every detail had become an imperative to Mom.

Mezuzahs—rolled up parchment inscribed with verses from the Torah inside small decorative cases—were attached to every door frame in our farmhouse and a small brass sign with black Hebrew letters hung from a wall of the dining room, a single word in Hebrew—east—pointing in the direction of Jerusalem. We abided by strict kosher dietary rules. That meant two sets of dishes, two sets of pots and pans, and two sets of utensils. And carefully stored away in the dining room closet, was a complete reduplication of the entire two-set arrangement for the eight days of Passover.

All this made me feel very whiny. "I'm the only kid in my class—maybe the whole school—who can't eat the cafeteria food," I said. Mom just ignored me. "The other Jewish kids can eat the school food."

"They're not religious. They're not kosher," she'd say.

Being Jewish was becoming a major stigma in school, making it all the harder to fit in with my classmates. Having to abide by the kosher laws just made it more intense. I wanted to be as American as everyone else. For heaven's sake, I thought, it's only food.

"I don't want to be different," I argued. "I want to be like the other boys."

"Well, you are different," was her final answer.

On Saturday, the Sabbath, all activities that might result in something breaking were forbidden. That meant no writing, cutting anything, driving, playing baseball, cooking, and even turning lights or appliances on and off. For a young boy the litany was overwhelming. Writing could result in breaking a pencil or tearing the paper;

driving was destructive in multiple ways; turning electrical circuits on and off could result in a fire; and sports were filled with all kinds of sinful possibilities. The baseball bat might break, the ball might hit someone, the basketball could get punctured, or a piece of clothing rip. I was living in the house of NO.

The only acceptable work was caring for the chickens or other livestock. Caring for people and animals was an authorized exception. Mom had to give on the electricity. She needed to find a Christian who would manage the switches but on a farm that didn't work, especially since we only had Jewish neighbors.

We did not go to Friday night or Saturday services since they were not available at the local synagogue but attending services was a must on all the high holidays. Walking was fine, just not driving. I tried to find an excuse for not walking but Mom scoffed at the idea that it could damage shoes. We had gone from being Germans to Orthodox Jews, all because of Hitler.

Mom often said, "Hitler taught me that we were not Germans—that we were Jews and I learned the lesson well."

Outside, at the back of the house, there were rows of chicken houses faced with white asbestos shingles, looking like a group of aging motel units; a white barn with an attached shed which was used as a garage for my father's blue Chevrolet sedan; and three old, gnarled, crabapple trees that were made for me to climb. My thrifty mother made tasty jam from the little, tart fruit.

A well dug deep in the ground—with a tar-paper pyramid cover—sat near the house. Water was piped from it into the house and out to the chicken coops. The water had a high iron content which, my mother pronounced, was the precursor to kidney stones. A few years later, we put in a shallower well with a red-handled pump

FARMINGDALE

FARMINGDALE OF THE LATE 1930s was a small town in central New Jersey with a cluster of old-fashioned stores, often named for the owners, some of which stand out in my memory because we knew the father or because I went to school with the kids. Megill's was a wood-frame, pine-plank-floored feed store with a potbellied stove and great bins and barrels and sacks of seeds and animal food as well as hardware in the dusty inside room. George Matthew's Chevrolet garage was located at the far end of town. Russell's candy store was also the public bus stop. It always seemed a forbidden place with a soda fountain and pinball machines—there was never any question that we had no money for such extravagances.

The Blue Moon Tavern, just outside of town, had an imposing sign. It was a strange place to me. The concept of a blue moon was baffling.

"What's a blue moon?" I asked Dad as we drove by.

"I never heard of such a thing," he answered. "I've never seen the moon blue."

"What's a tavern?" I persisted.

"It's not a nice place," he said, turning onto the West Farms Road. "We would never go there."

I turned around in my seat for one last glimpse at the

forbidden place. It was all very mysterious.

A five and dime and a grocery were of little interest to me. Lou ran the barbershop where, for years, I got all my haircuts. His back room, containing an array of pool tables, seemed dark and mysterious. We never visited the butcher shop since it did not sell kosher meat. The nearest kosher butcher store was ten miles away, in Freehold, the county seat. Farmingdale was surrounded by dairy and truck farms. They were the inner ring around the town. The chicken farms were further out. That's where we lived—three miles away.

Shopping was one of my father's great joys. As he bought all the farm supplies and did the grocery shopping, he had the opportunity to hone his English skills and visit with his new American acquaintances. His gregarious and genial nature made him popular with all the merchants. He asked about their families, laughed heartily at their stories, and was always kind and considerate. He was Sally to the world and everyone in this little local world liked him.

The chicken farms were latecomers to the established farming milieu of the community. Until the unsettling events in Europe began occurring, the farms were mostly truck farms that grew vegetables and fruit for restaurants and stores in the nearby towns and cities or raised milk-producing cows.

The traditional population was white and Christian—Presbyterian, Methodist, or Catholic. Except for a few Rosicrucians and Seventh Day Adventists (who tried to convert everyone), no one tried to influence us.

The big change for Farmingdale came in the 1920s with the influx of many Jewish immigrants. The early Jewish settlers were from Eastern Europe—Poland, Russia, Lithuania—escaping the poverty of the times as well as the anti-Semitism. The refugees of the 1930s, one another. When I announced one evening that he had done it in less than ninety seconds, even Mom had to restrain a smile.

It was more difficult for me to observe the orthodox rules and I rebelled early on. Mom and I had frequent arguments about the no driving, no sports, no biking or roller skating on Saturday (the Sabbath); issues on which she would later and often unexpectedly, compromise. And that was something we got on to, as Frank and I grew older. If there was a reason that could be presented as necessary to our future, we could often get our way. Practicing basketball and baseball (at which I had little skill, but what did Mom know?), became exceptions, since athletics were judged important for college entrance. By the time I was in high school, Friday night school events and Saturday track meets were rarely discussed. Frank followed and in time we boys went everywhere.

Mom was a lithe, slender, and attractive woman with a head of dark chestnut curls. Like most farmers' wives, she wore plain housedresses and heavy tan cotton stockings bought at the five and dime. She ruled at home with an iron hand, but in public she always deferred to my father's smooth and charming style. I still can't decide if she let him lead because it was expected of a woman, or was the reason for her reticence in public due to her lack of mastery of English?

She refused to learn how to drive for many years which limited her social contacts. When she finally tried it, I was in medical school. She promptly drove the car into one of the chicken houses. She wouldn't talk about it later but the large wood splinter driven through the front fender was irrefutable proof of the experiment. For once I didn't laugh; I could tell it was too sore a wound to open.

Farm work is exhausting and it was even more in those days before mechanization. It was an unbelievable change for my parents from their comfortable life in Dresden. It meant eighteen-hour days caring for the flock, collecting and cleaning eggs, repairing buildings and fences, shoveling manure, lifting heavy bags of feed and oyster shells. Mom helped with all these chores and also canned vegetables grown in our huge victory garden or bought at Bridgewater's truck farm nearby.

My father sat for hours each day in the basement at his worktable, cleaning each egg with a sandpaper brush—removing every last speck of dirt or dried manure. "It would certainly save lots of time if I just washed them," he would tell me in response to my obvious question, "but the dealers prefer this and pay me a premium price for doing it this way."

"But what's wrong with washing them?" I asked.

"They say a little of the water gets through the shell and spoils the quality," he answered.

After he'd cleaned each egg, he would weigh it on a small scale. Then he'd pack each one in the large egg cases according to size but he saved the jumbo double yolkers for his few private customers.

The white leghorn chicken is a hybrid variety that has an enormous capacity to produce eggs. The laying hen's pelvis is crammed with eggs in various stages of maturation. Once fully developed and covered with a hard calcium-based shell, they are ready to be laid. The eggs come in various sizes—small, medium, and large. The larger the egg, the more desirable it is, and the better the price. We used only the small eggs for ourselves. Mom and Dad favored them soft-boiled and eaten out of an egg cup. Frank and I liked them best scrambled.

"Let me show you how to really eat an egg," Dad said one morning.

I looked up from my cereal. What's the big deal, I thought. I'd seen the drill often enough. The egg was carefully placed in the egg cup. With a quick flick of Dad's wrist, the pointy top of the egg was neatly decapitated. A small tip of yellow yolk would show through, framed by the congealed egg white.

"This is what you do if you're someplace without an egg cup," Dad continued.

Okay, this sounds interesting, I thought.

He slipped off his gold wedding ring, laid it on the table in front of him, and placed the rounded bottom of the egg on it.

"If you let me draw a face on it," I said, "I can make it look like a king upside down, standing on his crown."

Mom brought over a piece of toast—I hardly noticed it was burned—and just shook her head. Gently, steadying the egg, he knocked off the lower part of the face of the imagined emperor. The egg sat securely on the ring as Dad began to scoop out its contents with a small egg spoon. Neat, I thought.

As I buttered my toast, I said, turning to Mom, "You let it burn, again."

"Mine is burnt, too," Frank chimed in.

Mom was in a good mood. "Let me tell you a story," she said. Mom was full of stories and aphorisms.

"There was a man who remarried after his first wife died. She was a good cook but could never make toast to the man's satisfaction. The new wife tried all different ways to prepare the toast but her efforts were always met with criticism."

"What's so hard about making toast?" Frank asked.

Mom ignored him and continued, "One morning, she was distracted and allowed the toast to burn. 'Aha,' the husband said, 'you finally got the recipe right.'"

"So?" I asked.

"It's what you get used to," she answered. "He missed the flavor of his late wife's toast. When you get older, you'll miss mine."

I thought the ring trick was better.

As I grew older, I marveled at the hours of solitude my father spent in the basement. Sometimes I'd go down to help him, sitting on the other side of the work table. He would weigh and pack the eggs I cleaned. We rarely talked. After an hour, I usually got bored and left. He didn't mind.

Dad was a powerful, muscular, sun-tanned man shaped like a fire hydrant. His hands were heavily calloused from the meticulous work and his arms powerful from throwing 100 pound sacks of feed about with little effort. He wore khaki pants, work shoes, and silk dress shirts, their removable collars long gone—shirts left over from an earlier time—and thin cotton feed-company caps.

My mother said admiringly, "He's a far cry from the overweight man he was in Germany. He was always sick with something but not anymore. Moving to America may have saved his life in more ways than just escaping the Nazis."

In the meantime, Great Britain, France, India, Australia and New Zealand declared war on Germany. The *Aufbau* reported on the same day, September 3, 1939, that David Ben-Gurion vowed that more than a million Jews would fight Hitler as soldiers in the armed forces of nations opposing Germany.

"I hope Roosevelt declares war soon," Dad said, his eyes tearing up.

EMILY MICHEL

IN LEAVING GERMANY, we lost a close-knit circle of family and friends. The loss was anguishing, especially since we feared every day for their lives. Leaving New York we again left relatives, but there was no concern for them, we only missed seeing them often. Our lives had always centered on family.

Since our farm was in the country and the surrounding neighbors were often Russian and Polish Jews whose ways of living were different from ours, we were only on polite terms with them. It took time but Mom and Dad gradually built a new circle based on mutual interests.

Dad made friends all over, as was his way. George Matthews, the car dealer, was the first but others followed, usually people he did business with.

Several of Mom's new friends were German Jewish immigrant farm wives, but her really close relationships were with local women who were not Jewish. Ironically, especially for Mom, her closest friends often turned out to be Christians.

Emily Michel was the first and that gave her a special status. We hadn't finished moving in but Dad knew he needed to buy a car. "There's only one place to go," another German farmer told him. "George Matthews sells

Chevrolets and, more important, he gives good service. You can't go wrong."

"Good service" resonated with Dad. In Germany, he'd been driven around in his chauffeur-pampered Chrysler. He knew a Chevy would be a step down but that didn't matter as long as it was reliable. The neighbor drove him into town.

The off-white, one story building at the end of Main Street had "George Matthews" and "Chevrolet – Sales and Service" emblazoned in blue above the plate glass showroom windows. It was easy to find.

"I want to buy a car," my dad said slowly in his heavily accented English. He wore a good pair of wool trousers and a white shirt, his tie neatly tucked into the top of his pants, not at all looking like the farmer he was about to become—but it was what Mom had insisted he wear. He had the substantial look of a successful businessman. "You have to make a good impression," she had said. He certainly did that.

A young woman slid slowly off her stool when Dad walked in the showroom. "It's nice to meet you," she said. "My name is Madeline Michel." She was overweight and walked with a pronounced tilt of her body, dragging her small left leg as if it were some extraneous object. But she said, with a warm and welcoming smile, "I'll get Mr. Matthews." A few moments later, George Matthews himself came back with Madeline.

They talked about new cars and Dad tried one out with George as passenger even though Dad didn't have a license. "Don't worry," George told him, "I'll drive you over to Freehold and we'll take care of that."

Dad was sure this was the place to buy a car and he and George quickly settled the deal. George looked pleased. He liked this new farmer who hadn't haggled over the price and was going to pay cash. He said he'd drive Dad home. They had become friends already.

Madeline watched as they discussed the car purchase. She too liked this new farmer. He was dressed neatly and was much more business-like than many of the other farmers who came looking at cars.

Dad stopped to thank Madeline as he was leaving. "My mother and I live on the way to your farm," she said. "I think she'd enjoy meeting you and your wife. She was born in Switzerland and likes people from Germany even though—I don't know how to say this"—she looked a little embarrassed, "they're doing so many bad things. Mr. Matthews will show you where the house is and my mother will call and invite you over. Her name is Emily,"

Like Dad, Emily Michel thrived on conversation and they were friends immediately. Mom was more cautious. This was the first American woman who had taken an interest in her and her family but she was a Christian. Mom wasn't so sure about Christians anymore, not since the debacle with German anti-Semitism. She had decided Christians were untrustworthy. Mom had non-Jewish friends in Germany but, as the Nazi era progressed, those friends gradually deserted her.

"I'm not sure I want to meet her," Mom said when Dad told her Emily would call, "but maybe you're right, maybe she could be helpful." After Mom met her, they hit it off right away. Perhaps she was responding to Emily's friendly and open ways and that she was from Switzerland. Being from Europe added a sense of kinship. Perhaps she knew we needed friends.

Emily Michel was one of those matriarchal women who enjoy helping others organize their lives. And Emily liked to talk. We heard about Emily's husband who worked as a night clerk at a New York City hotel and, their daughter, Madeline, and her terrible bout with polio as a small girl. She knew all the stores in the area and took

Dad and me around to Megill's Hardware Store and Louie's Barbershop in Farmingdale and she told him about the best stores in nearby Freehold.

At Megill's, Emily said she was sure I could come with Dad in the spring and help buy the seeds. Dad nodded his head.

Louie patted me on the head and said, "When you need a haircut, and that may be pretty soon, I'll be glad to give it to you."

Dad laughed, "We'll probably be back next week, maybe sooner."

Since Mom didn't go shopping she heard about our adventure from Dad. "Louie is going to give me a haircut soon," I announced. Mom smiled. She could see Emily's advice was good.

"When you need to buy vegetables in the summer, you see my friend, Ann Bridgewater. She's got the best beets, and cabbages, and corn. She even has kohlrabi and Brussels sprouts. And rhubarb."

Mom sent Dad to the Bridgewater farm a few weeks later. I went along for the ride. We had lived in the city in Germany and farms were still new to me. The rows and rows of vegetables amazed me. The cabbages had heads as big as a man; some bigger. The kohlrabies looked like giant spiders with huge tentacles. I liked looking at the little cabbages—the Brussels sprouts—growing up big tough stalks. Later I discovered eating them was another story.

Mom and I were visiting one day when the two women were inspecting Emily's berry garden. It was packed with raspberry, currant, and gooseberry bushes. Mom's hands were set firmly on her hips and Emily's arms folded over her ample bosom as they watched me trying to pick the first of the season's gooseberries.

Both women had been steeped in the old European

traditions but Emily had lived in America for twentyfive years and had long ago adopted the ways of the new world. "You must call me Emily," she said when they first met. Then, catching my attention, as I stood quietly near my mother, she added, "And when my husband is here from New York, Ludwig, you call him Uncle Sam."

"Emily?" Mom was tentative. "No, that's too hard. We never call friends by their first name."

"But, dearie, you are in America now," Emily said. "And, you must put in a garden; Megill's has all the seeds. Ludwig can help Sally dig it up but it needs some manure spread on it the week before. Then, looking at me again she added. "When the weeds start coming up you have get rid of them. You need a hand cultivator to help you and I just happen to have an extra one stored in my barn."

When she brought it out, Dad looked at the curved three-pronged steel tool with its long wooden handle in amazement. "I've never seen anything like it before. There's nothing like that in Germany."

Our victory garden became a perennial fixture on the farm. Each year there were tomatoes, potatoes, corn, cucumbers, lettuce, radishes, and cabbages to be planted and nurtured. The worst part of gardening, I discovered, was the constant need for pulling the ever-present weeds. I hated the job and some days it seemed beyond me. "I'll do it tomorrow," I'd say.

The answer was predictable—Mom would recite one of her favorite aphorisms. This one was a typical all-purpose one:

"Tomorrow, tomorrow, not today...
That's what the lazy people say."

I sighed. There was never a reprieve from Mom's constant moralizing.

Two years later, Emily and Mom were buddies. Mom turned to her for advice on everything she needed to have or to know. They discussed replacing the coal furnace with oil and which were the best washing machines. "I need to find a music teacher so Ludwig can begin violin lessons," Mom told Emily on one of their visits together. I wasn't sure I was very interested but I knew there was no escape once Mom made up her mind and Emily had nodded agreement.

"Rosi, you and Sally need to talk to Ann Bridgewater, she knows a couple of girls she really likes." By now we were regulars at the Bridgewater farm. Mrs. Bridgewater—Mom couldn't even think about calling her Ann—taught the sixth grade at Howell Township School. None of it sounded like a great idea to me, but at least it would get me out of feeding chickens and collecting eggs—or pulling weeds in the victory garden.

HILGERS

IT TOOK TWO YEARS, but in 1941, when I was eight, Mom came along on one of our forays to the Bridgewater farm to ask, as Emily had suggested, about music teachers for Frank and me. "I think you would like the Hilgers. They are such talented women," Mrs. Bridgewater told her. "They are the best in the area. They live together over on Route 9 but they'll come to your house for the lessons. I think they're Austrian."

"Austrian," must have sounded good to Mom. Despite her rejection of German society, she was still more comfortable with people who had similar customs.

A few weeks later, it was all decided over coffee and cake while sitting around the big table in the middle of our kitchen. The Hilger sisters, as they were always called, came over to meet us. Maria Hilger would take me on as her violin student and in a year, when Frank was old enough, he'd begin piano lessons with Gretel.

Music and literature were important to Mom and having her sons steeped in them was an imperative. "It is impossible to understand," she would say, sometimes in anger, at other times wistfully, "how such malevolent people like the Germans could have produced some of the greatest poets, authors, and composers in the world."

The classic mahogany bookcase that filled one wall of our living room contained many of the works of Goethe, Schiller, Heine, and Lessing.

Always judgmental, Mom considered Beethoven, Brahms, and Mendelssohn's works the epitome of greatness; and the anti-Semitic Wagner akin to the evil archangel. "Hitler loved his music. If Wagner had still been alive, he'd have been a Nazi." It was a statement of fact. There was no question in her mind.

Mom found the Hilgers to be first-rate teachers and they became her close friends. The sisters, despite being Christian, were given exalted positions in our household right from the start. Maria, her graying hair pulled neatly back behind her narrow face, was the older of the two and always serious, formal, and polite. Gretel, her hair tousled and her face rounder, was full of gossip and laughed loudly at the slightest provocation. Coffee and cake and discussions about our futures were regular weekly events after each lesson.

I started out using a three-quarter-sized violin but quickly graduated to a full-sized one. There were long discussions with the sisters about purchasing an appropriate quality violin as well as a good upright piano for Frank. Maria and Gretel, as music teachers often do, found the instruments for us and arranged the purchases.

Even though Mom addressed everyone, American and German friends alike, by their surnames, the Hilgers were always Maria and Gretel. Mom's relationship with them was special. First names were reserved for family and really close friends and that's how Mom saw them. Maria was like the older sister she never had and Gretel was everybody's pal. All of my mother's concerns about the present and the future were grist for the weekly late afternoon coffee klatch. Living on the farm away from town, and not being able to drive, my mother had little opportunity or time to make friends so these get-togethers were special for her.

Most of my violin lessons took place upstairs in my bedroom while Frank was demonstrating his ability on the piano in the dining room. Mom would bring one of the cushioned mahogany armchairs from her bedroom for Maria. I tuned my violin carefully before each lesson, opened the pieces I'd practiced and placed them on my aluminum music stand. This was serious business.

The music was full of notations from Maria as reminders for my afternoon practice sessions: "Think position, prepare for the next note, hold the violin higher, press fingers hard on the strings, and keep all your fingers on the bow and the bow arm up so you can look under it..." The instructions went on and on.

There would be bits of music philosophy written in: "Every major key has a 'poor sad' minor relative always found three steps below the major." I pictured the poor little rejected cousin standing sadly on the doorstep.

I always had questions for Maria, especially when my arms felt heavy in the middle of a lesson. I'd pause, lower my bow, and ask, "Why do they use all those words nobody ever heard of, like: tutti, poco allargando, dolce, largamente? Why do they have to write music with four flats? It's hard to play and it sounds gloomy."

Maria would just smile. She knew what I was up to. "Let's look at some new music. We have to keep playing. Your parents work hard to pay for your lessons."

"I don't like the Sevcik exercises as much as I do Wohlfahrt."

I knew that she had studied with Otakar Sevcik, but she just smiled. "They are hard," she said. "We can work on the Wohlfahrt." She never fell for my attempts to bait her into a time-wasting discussion.

Sometimes the lesson was at the Hilgers' house.

They lived only fifteen minutes away and Dad would drive me over. Off to one side was an Esso gas station run by their brother. Nobody ever talked about the brother except once, when Gretel said he was "unusual." No one ever seemed to stop for gas and I only saw him one time when Maria sent me over after a lesson to borrow a screwdriver. The room was dark and an unmade bed stood up against the far wall. Karl's face was hidden by a bushy beard. He wore a faded work shirt and grimy overalls and was slumped in a soiled stuffed easy chair. He looked at me with his face expressionless and pointed to a shelf.

The music room in the Hilger house was right off the front door. It was a light room with big windows. A large grand piano—"a Steinway," Mom always reminded me—monopolized the center of the room and was surrounded by plaster statues of Greek and Roman deities and huge flowerpots overflowing with plants. One wall had a series of glass doors that led into a dark living room.

There were never any unnecessary questions or attempts to stall during these lessons. They were all conducted under the stern and unyielding gaze of five large Dobermans. When I sat down, they would suddenly appear out of the blackness on the other side of the closed glass doors. The five would stand there the whole hour, legs apart, open mouths displaying large white teeth. They never moved, they never barked, and they never took their eyes off me.

"They are two single women living alone right on the main highway," Mom had told me. "They have no one to protect them, just those five dogs."

"There's Karl," I said.

Mom just harrumphed. I knew she thought the brother was useless.

I was just glad the glass doors were always shut. I felt a kinship with all the Grimm's fairytale characters faced with evil witches and wolves and was always relieved when the lesson at their house was over.

Maria and Gretel grew up in Austria during the early 1900s. With their younger sister, Elsa, who played the cello, they formed the Hilger Trio. When World War I ended, their mother brought them to the United States where they toured the country playing concerts during the 1920s and early 1930s. For years they lived out of suitcases, traveling by train or in their Buick on unpaved roads, and living in hotels. Their mother organized everything, made their clothes, and managed the finances.

The trio broke up in 1935 when Elsa was hired by Leopold Stokowski to play with the Philadelphia Philharmonic—the first time a woman was hired to be a full-time member of a major symphony orchestra. Maria and Gretel settled in their country house near Freehold to teach music.

As the years went by, Frank and I attained a level of proficiency that made us regulars on the local recital circles and I became concert master of the high school orchestra. The coffee interludes now dealt with the serious subject of my future (Frank was four years younger), and, in particular, if it was possible for a Jewish farm boy from a small-town high school to get into a university like Princeton. The sisters' friendship with Albert Einstein —for my mother, the epitome of the successful German Jewish immigrant—who was at Princeton's Institute of Advanced Studies, made them the oracles of hope. They still occasionally visited with him at Princeton—in years past the three sisters had regularly played quartets with him (Einstein playing the violin)—and he told them that Princeton was moving to a more diverse student body— so there seemed to be hope for me.

Just before I finished high school, Eugene Ormandy promoted Elsa to assistant principal cellist—the second chair in the cello section of the orchestra. A concert at the Academy of Music was to be a grand celebration for Elsa's admirers. We all drove to Philadelphia and listened enthralled from the first row in the balcony. Later, at the reception at Elsa's house, it was the unanimous opinion that Elsa played with much greater verve than the first chair. Elsa only smiled and reminded us that it was still a momentous occasion.

Later, the famous conductor observed, "You would have had the first chair but your pants were not long enough." The world of music has come a long way from those male-dominated days.

During high school, my becoming a professional musician was a serious question. There were many recitals where my performances received considerable acclaim.

The question was settled during my senior year.

As Frank and I sat quietly in the front row of the Freehold Women's Club, I thought about my career choices while the president discussed the agenda for the next meeting. I held my violin upright, the chinrest planted firmly on my thigh while my left hand held the neck of the instrument. My right hand held the bow loosely as it lay diagonally across my lap.

Mom watched me intently as I ran a piece of soft cotton cloth back and forth below the strings, removing the fine coating of rosin that collected on the wood. I'd rubbed the ribbon of white horsehair with my rosin block the day before and decided to skip doing it today. The strings were tuned and I was ready.

The agenda discussion was finally over and the matronly lady in charge announced that Frank and I would play for them and that we were students of Maria and Gretel Hilger. Frank took his place at the grand piano and opened the green covered music album. I stepped behind the metal music stand—I had adjusted its height earlier—and waited for Frank to strike the A key so I could retune my violin.

We were going to play Cesar Franck's *Sonata for Violin and Piano*. Our rehearsals had gone well with a minimum of brotherly bickering. Our disagreements usually revolved around the proper tempo of the piece, how loud each of us should be playing, and who should lead. The issues had been all ironed out the night before and we were ready to go.

I looked up. Mom and the Hilgers sat in the back row. In front of them were a few dozen older women sitting straight upright in their chairs, wearing hats that Uncle Friedl might have sold them.

I nodded to Frank and we began. As I brought the bow down on the strings for the long opening notes, I could feel the soft bounce that always occurred when I was nervous. I had played those notes smoothly and without the slightest tremor at home but now I had to concentrate on getting my right hand's subtle shaking under control. My left hand shook a little too but that only made my vibrato easier.

There's nobody out there, I thought to myself. It's just me and Frank. I glued my eyes to the music stand and never looked away. The tremor subsided during most of the piece but reappeared at the start of each movement.

Afterwards, over punch and cookies, everyone said it was wonderful. They congratulated Mom and the Hilgers and then talked about children, grandchildren, and events in town.

On the way home, sitting in the back seat with Mom and Frank, I said, "I'd have done better if my bow hadn't bounced so much. It never happens at home—just when I'm on a stage."

Maria, driving the car, turned her head toward me, "I hardly noticed it. It's because you're a little nervous.

It'll get better when you're older."

"My hands never shake," Frank piped in.

Mom turned to Frank who was sitting on her other side, "You are like your father. You both have steady hands. I get a little shaky too when I'm nervous. Your brother gets that from me."

"If both boys keep practicing as they do, they can be first class musicians," Gretel said. My reverie had come to an end.

Mom didn't say anything but I knew what she was thinking, it was the same litany, her mantra, "You must have skills that you can take with you when the next wave of anti-Semitism occurs. Having to move is the history of the Jews. We have always had trouble, wherever we were. Even here in America you have to prepare yourself to emigrate. Your father and I were born in Germany and we thought we were real Germans but Hitler changed all that."

I knew the speech—I'd heard it often enough. She would continue, "Look at the Hilger sisters. They came to the United States from Austria with their mother and had no trouble continuing their music careers. Just look at my cousin, Mille, her husband was a doctor in Germany and now he's a dermatologist in New York. And being a scientist is good. Look at Albert Einstein. He had no trouble getting a job at Princeton."

For good measure she would have added, "And don't forget what happened to Otto Goldstein, a federal judge in Germany and now he's a chicken farmer here, just like your father. Being a lawyer is just as bad as being a business man."

Once I had said, "Maybe I should be a rabbi," Mom laughed with disbelief.

"You?" she said. "It would be an honor for all of us but, no, music or being a doctor would be better for you."

I came out of my reverie to hear Maria tell Mom the latest news about her sister, Elsa, and the Philadelphia Philharmonic Orchestra. I worried about the goal of being a professional violinist. The bouncing bow on stage was a problem. It had even happened at the beginning of a concert by the high school orchestra. Mom seemed to say I'd gotten it from her. I'd seen her hands tremble when she was upset—even her head shook a little once in a while. I took a quick look at her. Even now her curls seemed to vibrate. Maybe it was just the car. I reached up and touched my hair. Everything was quiet. I held up my right hand—it was quiet too.

I'd never thought about my tremor being an inherited problem like my brown eyes and brown hair. Years later, I would learn that it was called familial tremor and that Frank and I each had a fifty percent chance of acquiring the abnormal gene from Mom. I was the lucky one.

I would also learn that the tremor is rarely disabling but interferes with fine motor activity, especially of the hands. It is always worse with stress and that was already evident in my difficulty controlling the violin bow at recitals. This realization would influence my career choices although the decision was never a conscious one. The drug, propranolol, would turn out to be effective in damping down my tremor but that was still many decades in the future.

Perhaps I could be a violinist if I tried harder but the seeds of doubt were beginning to sprout. At that moment I could see science or medicine as a better bet.

BECOMING AN AMERICAN

WHEN I WAS A LITTLE KID, if someone had asked me, "Where are you from?" I would have looked surprised and answered, "I'm from here, from Farmingdale."

"No. no. I mean are you German or American?"

The question would have confused me. Small children live in the moment and exist in their own worlds. At first, they don't see themselves belonging to groups. Identifying with certain clusters of people develops later in their young lives.

The idea that I might be German would never have crossed my mind, even though I knew I was born in Germany. I knew that the Americans were good guys in the war and that the Germans and Japanese were bad but Dad having been a soldier in World War I for the Germans had no real significance for me.

For my parents, their being German must have been a struggle. They had been Germans all their lives and were steeped in the culture and language. Despite their anger about being rejected and needing to emigrate, they were still Germans trying to make a transition.

In a moment of resentment, Mom would declare, "We are not Germans. We are German Jews. Now, there is a difference."

In reality—from a technical point of view—my parents, as well as Frank and I, were a family without a country during those early years in the United States. We were no longer considered Germans, but we're not yet American citizens.

At first it was by inference. The Nuremberg Race Laws became German law in 1935, depriving Jews of our rights of citizenship and giving us the status of "subjects" in Hitler's Reich. Because of this law, to be a German citizen meant that all four grandparents had to be of "true German origin." Even one Jewish grandparent meant an individual was contaminated and could not be considered a "pure" German. The law also prohibited marriage or sexual intercourse between Jews and Aryan Germans. The disenfranchised state of the Jews was formalized by the Nazis in 1941 with the "Eleventh Decree to the Law on Citizenship of the Reich." This act stripped German citizenship from all Jews including those living in other countries.

The *Aufbau* reported on the new regulations in detail. Of course, none of it mattered to me in the least. As Dad pointed out, "It doesn't really make a difference to us; we have already disassociated ourselves from Germany. We have asylum in this country. Our future is here."

Mom was more direct. Her statements were often all-encompassing and thus useful in all situations as far as she was concerned. "Those Germans, they're just a bunch of *Verbrecher*—criminals."

Becoming a United States citizen was one of Dad's first goals. He recognized the value of citizenship while Mom seemed too consumed with her anger toward Germany to care. At Dad's urging, however, they bought a book on American history and studied it after dinner for several months. The evening before the exam he was still worried he'd be asked questions for which he had no answer.

When Dad went to the Freehold courthouse to become an American, he took his car dealer and close friend, George Matthews, with him. He didn't really need a witness but George provided emotional support. Dad had just returned home when the school bus pulled up in front of the house. I ran down the driveway and into the house, clutching my books.

"Are you a citizen?" I asked, breathlessly. I knew how important it was to him and now it had become important to me.

He was beaming when he announced, "The only thing the judge asked me was whose picture was on the penny and who was on the dollar. I told him it was Abraham Lincoln and George Washington."

It was a major event. Afterwards, he and George had a celebratory midday dinner and cocktails at the American Hotel, right across the street from the county courthouse. The hotel was an old three story wood structure reminiscent of the Revolutionary War era. It stood in sharp contrast to the modern concrete courthouse. The hotel was the fanciest place to eat in Freehold.

Mom had quietly become a citizen a few months before. Emily Michel took her to the courthouse and when she came home, she went right back to her work. The only big dinner she had was the one she made for us that evening.

I remembered a picture from one of my German children's books. A fish is watching a chicken celebrating after laying a single egg. The fish smiles and shakes her head in wonder. "There would be an unbelievable racket if I did that over every egg I produce," she says. Working with the hens is rubbing off on Dad, I thought.

But as I pictured the celebration—the big dinner and the cocktails—my excitement turned to outrage. I confronted Mom, parroting what I had expected her to say.

"How could we afford such an expensive thing? And he had a sirloin steak that wasn't kosher..."

To my surprise, Mom smiled wistfully. "When you grow up a little more, you'll understand."

I was impressed. I was sure she'd find fault with him as she often did, especially over the non-kosher steak. Mom was an opinionated, tough-minded woman who rarely wavered in her determination—this was an inexplicable diversion from the norm she had set up as law.

"Don't worry yourself," she continued. "It was important that Mr. Matthews went with your father. He's a busy man who did this as a special favor. We had to show him that we appreciated it."

"What about me and Frank?" I asked. "When do we have to take the test?"

"You and your brother are now American citizens because of us," she smiled. "When we became citizens, you did, too. You'll get your own citizenship paper in Newark—but only when you are old enough to need it. Don't get all excited, you two shouldn't expect a test and a big party; it's automatic."

AUFBAU

AUFBAU—the word means reconstruction—was a weekly German language newspaper, founded in 1934, that catered to the immigrant German Jewish population living in New York and New Jersey. It was published by the New World Club in New York City and was my parents' major contact with the news in our early years of living in America. For the readership of the *Aufbau*, Germany was their past and the United States, their future. It was both comforting and upsetting for them to read the news in German and to focus on what was happening to other German Jewish immigrants in this and other countries and the worsening disaster for those who had stayed in Germany.

My father walked down the gravel driveway just a little quicker on Thursday when he knew the *Aufbau* would be waiting in the mailbox on the other side of the dusty dirt road. A car shrouded in yellow dust coming down the eroded, washboard surface of Richard Road at noon was likely to be the mailman. Dad would stop what he was doing and walk the fifty yards to meet him.

I remember the cartoon section. These drawings were not like the ones in the American newspapers, where a generation of political and family humor was typified by the relaxed approach of Bill Mauldin's, G.I. Joe and H. T. Webster's, Mr. Milquetoast. In the *Aufbau*, the European-style political drawings were filled with pointed and sardonic humor. Their more abstract, sharp-edged drawing style is still popular in Germany.

The newspaper was full of tips for the Jewish immigrants—how to adjust to life in America, preparing for citizenship exams, and job opportunities. What interested us the most, however, was the news from Germany and the work to establish Israel as an independent Jewish state. Albert Einstein and Thomas Mann, both German émigrés, were frequently featured. Their writings appealed to the highly-educated readers.

The worsening anti-Jewish activities of the Nazis were meticulously reported. The details of Kristallnacht, with the destruction and vandalism of innumerable synagogues, the ransacking of thousands of Jewish businesses and homes, and the arrest and incarceration of more than 30,000 Jewish men were highlighted in detail by the paper.

Mom read the accounts with mounting fury. "We wouldn't have had a chance in Germany," she said and as her anger increased, she added, "The damned Germans are evil. Sometimes it's even hard to admire their culture. We are well rid of them."

As it turned out, Opa, Mom's dad, was caught in the midst of *Kristallnacht*. A Christian neighbor warned him the previous afternoon that his home would be looted. Opa collected his valuable belongings into a leather bag and slept that night in a culvert just outside of town.

The next day, Ernst drove down from Frankfurt looking for Opa. Ernst found him standing, dazed, a hopeless look on his face, in front of his home. The grape vines had been torn down and all the windows broken. Inside, the house was a shambles. Cabinets were overturned, furniture destroyed, and large swastikas drawn on the walls.

Opa felt helpless. Ernst collected the leather bag from the ditch and Opa left his hometown of Schlierbach forever.

The *Aufbau* was the first to describe the news about the concentration camp gas chambers. Dad cried and Mom was consumed with horror and anger.

"All I can think of is I hope Rosel and Julius and the girls can find a way to escape," she said as she rummaged through her collection of pictures to find a snapshot of my three cousins. In this formal portrait, they stand together, barely smiling at the camera. "There they are only a year ago, I wonder where they are now? We'll frame this and put it in the living room." She knew we would never see them again. I looked seriously at the picture. I couldn't remember them but I knew they were important.

After the war was over, the *Aufbau* printed lists of Holocaust survivors. Each week, Dad went through the list meticulously looking for his sister and her family. In the end, it was all a futile effort. Mom's premonition was correct. We never heard from them again.

The death announcements appearing toward the back of the paper were the most remarkable feature of the *Aufbau*. They were nothing like the obituaries of today. The newspaper term "tombstone ad" comes from the look. They were paid, formal messages in different styles and sizes, some with ornate borders, often designed to look like the gravestones in a cemetery. The announcements would begin: "We wish to announce the death of our honored husband and father..." Close relatives of the deceased were listed. Many of the announcements were an eighth of a page but others were larger.

My father read these notices with the interest of one of our hens after grain—going after every one. It was a weekly ritual. He learned about the death of some acquaintance, that he and his family had escaped, and where they had settled in America. This information made the obituary column a major feature—keeping people in touch, even in death.

My father would read the announcements out loud at the kitchen table while Mom prepared dinner, telling my mother about people they had known. I would sit at rapt attention listening to the stories they told.

"I don't remember him," Mom would say.

"Of course you do," Dad would answer. "We met them the year before we left. We were on our vacation in the Harz Mountain. He owned a rug factory and he had that young wife with flaming red hair who just fell all over Ludwig."

Mom nodded her head. She'd remembered.

"He died in New York."

"I'm glad they escaped the Nazis," Mom would say.

Cemeteries are interesting cultural phenomena. Anthropologists look for them as civilizing signs in early societies. They are a way to honor and remember a dead family member. And there is comfort in having the grave in the community in which the person has lived. It was desirable to be buried near loved ones—it meant returning home.

The German Jews of my parents' age, like other immigrants, would often die in America, separated from their friends and even their family, in strange new communities where they were outsiders and not always well accepted. While they were glad to be out of the danger pervading Germany, and despite their angry feelings about their old country, a part of them missed the familiarity of home. The *Aufbau's* death announcements were a formal way to reconnect with their old life in the old world. For a young boy growing up in New Jersey, this bond with my family's past seemed unique.

The Daily Worker

BEING JEWISH IN FARMINGDALE was always difficult. When we first moved there, I was six and it was the simple issue of some of the Christian boys bullying me, the only Jewish boy in the class. The girls had little interest in the harangues or the fights. Being German was synonymous with being Jewish and I didn't want to be either one. I just wanted to be American—not different.

By the time I became a teenager, it was all much more complicated. On the one hand being Jewish was no longer an issue in high school—no one seemed to care. Some of the teachers were Jewish and, since it was a regional high school and students came from all over the county, more of the kids were, too. Sports, dating, music, and cars were much more important than religious affiliations.

Still, being Jewish was a major focus at home and it was becoming more complex. There were the German Jews on the one hand and the Polish and Russian Jews on the other. The Germans viewed themselves superior to the Eastern European Jews. Those from the eastern countries had come from peasant backgrounds with little formal education, in contrast to the German families who had strong educational and cultural backgrounds.

It is probably not surprising that the people from

Eastern Europe were often less meticulous than the Germans. That was visible in their homes, their front lawns, their fences, and even the repair of their chicken houses. The neatness of the German farms went unmatched and so was their sense of superiority. We were the only German Jewish family within several miles and Mom had nothing good to say about our Jewish neighbors. That fed into my isolation since, no surprise, I had no neighborhood friends.

With the end of the war the influence of Communism on American institutions and the threat of Soviet espionage became an increasing concern in the media, fueled by the investigations and denunciations of Senator Joseph McCarthy. The doctrines of Communism and Socialism were of little interest to most of the people of Farmingdale —except for the eastern Jews.

"There's enough anti-Semitism in the world," my mother said, "and now our neighbors are going to make it worse by singing the praises of Communism."

"The capitalist system is better than Communism and Stalin has always been a big anti-Semite," Dad said. "I don't understand why the Russian farmers like him so much. Even when we still lived in Germany, he had all the purges against the Russian Jews."

"Maybe they forgave Stalin because his children all married Jews," Mom answered, a tinge of sarcasm in her voice.

"Is that really true?" I asked.

Mom nodded her head.

"The *Aufbau* said he personally arranged for Leon Trotsky's murder," Dad said.

"I'm not surprised," Mom said. "Trotsky was just another Jew to him."

"I saw Mr. Abramsky reading the *Daily Worker* when I was at Matthews' garage," Dad said, changing the subject.

"What's the *Daily Worker*?" I wanted to know.

"It's the newspaper published by the Communist Party," Dad answered. "It wants to bring Communism to America."

"Americans don't want Communism," Mom added. "That paper is not written for us. It's their newspaper," I knew she meant our neighbors. "It's the *Aufbau* that has respected writers like Albert Einstein, Thomas Mann, and Stefan Zweig."

More and more, I heard about Communism infiltrating American society on the radio and on the school bus. Tagora and Ruth were two girls in my high school class who lived on farms near ours. They always got on the bus together, since their farms were next door to each other.

Bus conversations could become heated. I was always being "told" about politics. "Communists and Socialists are concerned about everyone's welfare," Tagora would explain. "They believe in equality for everyone."

"But America is already about equality. And it's about freedom for everyone. We all have the right to vote and do what we want. It's all in the Constitution and the Bill of Rights." I said.

"Look at all the poor and needy people in New York," Ruth said, glaring at me. "That's exploitation of the masses by the rich—the Rockefellers and the DuPonts. If Lindbergh had his way, he'd have sent you back to Adolph Hitler."

The discussions went on morning after morning. Tagora seemed to tolerate me, trying to win me over with facts. Ruth was often angry.

"Look at the *Daily Worker*," I said. "It's run by the American Communist Party and supports Stalin. The editor just got accused of recruiting agents for the Russian secret service."

"That's a lot of propaganda," Tagora said. "The *Daily*

Worker supports collective ownership of our industries and is against private ownership. It wants to help the poor."

"And as far as your Bill of Rights and freedom of the press goes," Ruth snapped, "It's harder and harder to buy the *Daily Worker*." She paused. "Thanks to that Senator from Wisconsin."

"Maybe it's hard to get because they don't have any good writers like the ones who write for *The Aufbau*."

"You think Woody Guthrie's not good?" Ruth quickly countered.

That stopped me. I was beginning to admire his songs about the poor and downtrodden in our country. As a singer, he was an eloquent spokesman for their plight. He would become one of my favorite all-time singers.

The tension between the United States and the Soviets kept escalating. The anti-Semitic attacks at Howell Township School were not repeated in high school but I worried that Communism would be viewed as a Jewish phenomenon and the attacks would flare up again.

When I mentioned it to Mom, she said, "The boys are too busy running after girls now to be bothered chasing after anybody else." She paused. "Just make sure you keep bringing home all those A's." For Mom it was all about grades and excelling in music. "Your father and I want you to go to a good university. That's especially important for a Jewish boy."

"So, what do you think of this McCarthy guy?" Ruth asked after getting on the bus one day. "He says the State Department is run by Communists. Do you believe that?"

"I don't know," I answered. "I hope he's wrong."

"Well, he is wrong," she said. "He's calling anyone a Communist who's in favor of labor unions and against big business interests."

I kept thinking about Woody Guthrie and all the

poor unfortunate people in America. At least they had a chance here; I didn't think they did in Russia. "I still think Stalin is a bad person and that Communism is not for us."

Ruth swiveled in her seat and stared out the window.

THE SYNAGOGUE

THE JEWISH COMMUNITY CENTER in Farmingdale, nestled in a wooded area on the Peskin Road two miles from our farm, was converted into a synagogue during the Jewish High Holy Days. It was an old gray building that hadn't seen a coat of paint in a decade.

"It looks like a real old building," I said to Dad, on the way home from our first holiday service. "One of the kids said it used to be a one room schoolhouse."

"It is old," Dad said. "It was built more than ten years ago. But it never was a schoolhouse. The farmers that were here then, built it themselves. It isn't much but they did their best."

The inside was a single large room with light gray walls devoid of any decorations—no drapes hid the dust-covered windows. The drabness of the room served to highlight the Ark that stood in a central spot along one wall.

The Ark was a large cabinet with folding doors neatly covered with a shiny red silk-velvet curtain with Hebrew letters elegantly stitched in gold. It was beautiful to my young eyes. The curtain served to protect and venerate the two sacred Torahs that stood carefully placed in the cabinet, leaning against its walls.

The men sat around several long tables, which were placed along the sides of the room. The Ark stood between two of the tables against one of the long walls. Across the room, in a corner near the door, were two tables with benches for the women. The tables and benches were made of rough-hewn wood, simply constructed and gray from years of aging.

The women were segregated so as not to distract the men from the important rituals and prayers they conducted. A large, heavy, wooden table, twice the size of the others, stood in the center of the room. This table was where the elders led the service and where the Torah was reverently laid and unscrolled for the weekly reading. A red velvet cloth, matching the Torah curtain, with fringes hanging from the edges, covered the unfinished wood tabletop.

The colorless simplicity of the building and its contents matched the personality of the community it served—hard working immigrants eking out their livelihoods on small nearby farms. The rich red velvet of the Ark, the Torah covers, and the prayer table symbolized their hopes and aspirations.

The Torah reading was for me the high point of the service. The message, chanted in Hebrew, was beyond my understanding. It was the fascination of observing the right to read the various sections being auctioned— watching the farmers compete for the privilege to read. The bidding by the men was performed under the attentive eyes of their wives who paid close attention to how much their husbands were willing to spend.

The auctioneer was the shammes—the equivalent of the sexton in Christian churches. He would always ask the high bidder in a mixture of Hebrew and English, "*Alef* (one) dollar for the shammes?" The response was always, "Yes." My mother always made sure Dad did not exceed the amount agreed upon at Friday's dinner, including the dollar.

The shammes was Mr. Gottesfeld—he must have had a first name but no one ever used it. He was always Mr. Gottesfeld. A tall, slightly hunched-over man, he lived with his equally elderly wife in a ramshackle house. He didn't have a car or truck. He walked through the neighborhood, several miles every day, pulling a wagon in which he collected other people's junk—a radio that didn't work, a broken shovel, a hammer lying along the road. His backyard gave testimony to his being a junk collector.

He was the poorest man in the area. A Polish immigrant, he could neither read nor write. Mom told me that when he got married years ago, he and his new wife used an old wooden door supported by two saw bucks as their honeymoon bed. As far as I knew—and Mom was my source of information—the only income he had was the few dollars he made as the shammes and whatever he could get from selling his junk. Sometimes Dad took him along on a trip to nearby Freehold for shopping.

We always attended the Rosh Hashanah and Yom Kippur services. Mom's imposed driving restrictions applied to these high holy days. Much to my dismay, we had to walk the two miles back and forth.

"You can walk," I said, "but I'd rather ride my bike."

"No riding of any kind on the high holy days," Mom countered.

Predictable. I couldn't even kick the stones in the road as we went along—"No breaking anything," my Mother would warn as we set out.

The Jewish Community Center was much more than a synagogue although I was only vaguely aware of its other activities. It served as social gathering place for the Jewish farmers and their families and had a Yiddish school for the children.

Mom not only was distrustful of the Christian community, she was critical of our eastern Jewish neighbors. Their lack of education, their unkempt personal appearances, and the ramshackle and dilapidated look of their farms belied the cleanliness and orderliness that my mother so highly prized.

You might think that these immigrants wearing European clothes, speaking with heavy foreign accents, and moving into a rural white Anglo-Saxon farming community, would naturally band together. The Eastern Europeans did exactly that, building the community center that served as both a place to gather for social events and a synagogue, just as they had in their small Eastern European villages.

But the cultural divide between the German Jews and the Eastern European Jews was enormous. And because German Jews were uncommon in New Jersey farm country—almost as rare as males in a brooder house full of baby chicks—there were not enough people to build Synagogues and schools. Also, the Germans were well educated and accustomed to being part of the general public. Our German friends had been businessmen, engineers, attorneys—one had even been a federal judge. The education of their children was of primary importance to them and assimilation into the larger society was the way to succeed in this new country.

Our Eastern European neighbors had grown up in ghettos and had little education beyond a few years of Jewish and Hebrew studies. Many of these farmers spoke little or no English and still clung to their traditional Yiddish language. They had been laborers, shopkeepers and tradesmen. Their children's help on the farm—essential for the family's survival—was considered the first priority. Education was often not paramount.

We had a neighbor named Gertrude Wishnick who

lived less than a half mile from our farm although I barely knew her. I learned more of her years after we had left
the area. There were two reasons for the lack of contact:
she was seven years older than I and she and her family
were Eastern European Jews. Mom discouraged me from
playing with the neighborhood children, as if their souls
were as shabby as their personal appearance and the look
of their farms.

In her scholarly book, *The Land Was Theirs* (University
of Alabama Press, 1992, p. 205), Gertrude described the
differences in Jewish life in Farmingdale:

> *"I knew that the new arrivals in Farmingdale were
> German Jews, but I did not know they were refugees. I
> found it strange that they did not speak Yiddish; to me,
> Yiddish was synonymous with being Jewish. Nor did their
> children attend the Yiddish shule, which met on weekends.*
>
> *"I saw them only on the High Holy Days of Rosh
> Hashanah and Yom Kippur, when the Community Center
> became a synagogue. They greeted people cordially and
> politely, sat quietly during the service, shook hands with
> those near them when they left, wished people a good year,
> and retired until the following Rosh Hashanah. The only
> community activity in which they participated, as far as I
> could determine, was the United Jewish Appeal. But even
> in the brief encounters we had, I could see they were dif-
> ferent from the others.*
>
> *"Everything about these newcomers said 'culture' and
> 'education'. They always looked neat and clean; their
> clothes fit them well and looked expensive. Our closest
> German neighbors, the Gutmanns, kept their farm in
> immaculate condition. The outbuildings looked as if they
> were freshly painted every year; flowers and shrubbery
> were neatly trimmed. There was not the same wild profu-
> sion of bushes on their grounds as on ours. For all that one*

could see or smell, there were no chickens, even though we knew the Gutmanns were farmers. Their two sons did not seem to have farm chores to do after school, unlike the rest of us. They had to study their school lessons and practice their violins [sic]. The fact that, at a young age, they were preparing for college and a future professional life made them different from the other Jewish children I knew."

Gertrude Wishnick Dubrovsky PhD proved herself to be an unusual woman and far ahead of her time and her background. Determined to go to college, she fought her family and the traditions of her culture and attended Georgian Court College, ultimately receiving a doctorate degree from Columbia University.

old man but, unlike our neighbor, he had a long scraggly grey beard like one of those ancient rabbis I'd seen in Mom's picture books.

I'd seen dead chickens before and had watched the cats hunt for mice and kill them. Watching a shochet at work seemed an exciting adventure.

I was in for a surprise.

I helped Dad lift the wooden crate holding a white feathered chicken out of the car trunk. It hadn't been ill—that would have made it not kosher, not appropriate to be cooked—but it had an injured leg that made it a target to the rest of the flock. Chickens, especially those confined in coops, are cannibalistic and defects in others will set them off to attack the injured one.

The chicken was frightened, squawking and pooping at the same time. I wanted to go over to the crate to reassure it but, instead, I stayed frozen in a corner of the yard.

The old man came out of the garage and nodded at Dad. I could hear the crinkling of the straw as he silently walked to the center of the yard. No words were exchanged. It was a well-practiced weekly ritual and my being there seemed to escape his notice. His wrinkled white shirt was loosely tucked into his black trousers, his yarmulke sat askew on his balding head. He held a black velvet covered box in his left hand. Opening it, he carefully lifted out the knife, called the challef, its broad blade reflecting the bright morning sunlight. He carefully ran a finger across the blade's cutting edge, making sure it was razor-sharp and free of any nicks or dents.

My gaze never left the bearded man and his gleaming knife. The chicken kept up its frantic squawking. How does it know something bad is about to happen, I wondered?

Dad told me that killing the chicken had to be done in a carefully prescribed manner. Death had to be instantaneous—the chicken should feel no pain and was not allowed to suffer. This required one quick stroke across the neck, skillfully severing all the blood vessels, nerves, trachea, and esophagus.

Dad handed the hen to the unsmiling old man. No one spoke—only the persistent clucking of the hen broke the morning stillness. The old man skillfully tucked the fluffy white body under his left arm and, with two fingers grasped the red comb, pulling the head back. He quickly plucked a few fluffy feathers on the neck and deftly sliced through it, dropping the bird on the straw. It all happened in the blink of an eye. The chicken, its head dangling to one side and blood squirting everywhere, landed on its feet and ran around in a frenzy of automatic muscle movements for a few seconds before collapsing.

Suddenly, the chicken had gone from its frantic cackling to a limp mass of crimson stained fluff. I looked more carefully at the surrounding straw. The red speckles that covered the straw were from other animals killed by the old man.

Dad paid the shochet and picked up the now immobile chicken by its feet and put it back in the crate and loaded it into the trunk. All this time I stood to one side and didn't help. I was still a bit short of breath from the instant death and the unexpected ending.

We climbed in the car and I turned, looking out the back window. The bearded man was putting the broad bladed knife back in its box. I shuddered as I watched him disappear into his garage. I was glad he was gone.

I didn't speak until we had driven a good way down the road. "Does he do anything else for a living," I asked.

"No," Dad answered. "He's busy being a shochet."

The visit to the butcher went quickly. The large clump of sausages in the display case drew my attention. I imagined they had once been little animals whose heads had been lopped off in the straw-covered yard.

We walked across the street to the drug store. Before we left Dad asked, "Do you want an ice cream cone?" Dad must have known an ice cream cone was such an unusual treat it could heal any unpleasant experience.

When I said yes, he said, "Good, but don't tell your mother." I knew she would think it an extravagance.

Once we got home with all our purchases and the dead chicken, Dad took it out to the barn where he expertly plucked off all the feathers. Then Mom took over, opening the abdomen to remove the organs as it lay on an old wooden work bench. By this time my usual nosy nature had returned and I was again interested in the process. Mom had cleaned chickens many times before but I had never noticed until now.

She took out the heart and lungs, then the gizzard, and, finally, a huge coil of intestines, her hands moving as effortlessly as those of the shochet. What remained—and seemed to fill most of the abdominal cavity—were the ovaries and a series of developing eggs. There were tiny yolks, medium sized ones, and even two fully developed eggs whose shells were still soft.

Mom sensed my astonishment. "White leghorns are little egg factories," she said. "That's what they are bred to do—lay eggs."

Although farm children are often very matter-of-fact about death, this chicken in its terror had become special to me. Chickens were not bright, I knew that. I had tried to make several into pets with no success but this chicken and I had been through a lot today.

"You know," I said, "we sure went to a lot of trouble to kill that chicken. It might have been better if we did like the neighbors—just chop the head off with a hatchet. It seems to work just as well and doesn't cost anything." And it didn't seem quite as barbaric.

"It wouldn't be kosher, the hatchet might be dull and the chicken might suffer..." she answered, straightening up (a signal that question-time was over), "Besides, you need to go inside and practice your violin."

I saw the chicken with its heart, gizzard, and liver again later that evening, in the kitchen. It lay in a wire basket carefully placed on top of a bucket under the sink, all pink puckered skin, no feet, and not a single feather. The hen was naked except for a coating of rock salt—out of a red and yellow box marked "strictly kosher"—that was meant to drain any blood left in the carcass and the organs. Removing all the blood was also the purpose of the having the shochet kill the chicken and using the salt finished the job. At least, so Mom thought, and would have Frank and me believe.

At the moment, though, Frank was distracted by a black fly buzzing around the kitchen. He was trying to whack it with a fly swatter that Dad kept in a closet.

"Stop that," Mom yelled, as a water glass crashed onto the floor. Frank ran out of the kitchen fast, escaping Mom's fury.

I looked up at the ribbon of yellow fly paper hanging from the overhead light. It was studded with flies, some immobile, others struggling vainly to unglue themselves. Mom followed my direction of gaze.

"Between the broken glass on the floor and that awful looking fly paper..." she said. "Sally, I think it's time for me to sweep up and you to put up a new roll."

I turned my attention back to the remains of the squawking hen, its feathers replaced by a shroud of crystalline salt, carefully framed in Mom's wire basket. Dad watched me, knowing no good could come from my careful inspection. I suddenly realized I didn't want to eat that chicken or the soup that Mom would cook. Besides,

I already disliked hearts, gizzards and liver.

I couldn't leave it alone. "Do you really think this gets all of the blood out?" I asked Mom just before Dad turned on the radio to listen to Gabriel Heatter's news program.

All I got from Mom was a firm, "Yes," as Dad turned up the radio and Heatter's voice drowned me out. "Good evening, everyone—there's good news tonight."

More About Chickens

CHICKENS EXISTED ON OUR FARM for one reason only and that was to lay eggs. That was all we asked of them. The eggs were our primary product. Selling the hens for stewing after two years as their productivity waned and developing fertilized eggs for a local hatchery were very secondary—and almost incidental—but good sources of revenue.

The chickens were called White Leghorns. They were a breed developed solely for their ability to produce up to 300 eggs per chicken per year throughout their egg-laying time. When their ability declined, between their second and third years of life, we sold them to a chicken meat dealer. By then they were old hens and, while tasty, too tough for anything but fricassee or soup. The income of the farm depended on selling eggs and Dad kept detailed records on the productivity of each flock of chickens.

The farm business was specialized. New Jersey was known for "truck farms," where fruit and vegetables were raised. They supplied Manhattan restaurants and produce markets. Then there were egg farms like ours that specialized in eggs, while a few farms raised frying and roasting hens. There were also farms that supported the chicken business—hatcheries that produced chicks.

Fuzzy yellow baby chicks arrived early each spring from Henry Rapp's hatchery. Henry made sure they were all females. He had a near-perfect record but there would always turn out to be a couple of males that got through the screening process.

Over dinner one night, Dad announced, "I tried to tell the difference but I can't see it. They are such tiny creatures. No wonder Henry's man gets paid a lot."

The chicks traveled in flat, rectangular boxes and were kept in our brooder house, a long building divided into six rooms. Each room contained a large hooded stove (initially coal, but later electric), to keep the chicks warm.

The minute chicks grew quickly and their fine yellow fluff was soon replaced by long white feathers. They ate finely ground corn and wheat and drank water from low-to-the-floor fountains.

By early summer they were moved out into a big fenced-in field called a range. The area had to be large enough—several acres—for more than one thousand chickens. At night they slept in wood framed structures with peaked wooden roofs and sides enclosed by chicken wire called shelters. There were ten shelters spread widely apart. Each sat on a raised wire-covered frame over a manure pit. The frame was large enough to hold all the summer's chicken droppings. Corn and wheat was spread on the ground every afternoon from our truck. Water was piped to strategically-placed water fountains.

There seemed to be few natural predators, although we had a fox scare at one time and a hawk would occasionally carry off a bird when they were out running around and nibbling insects on the range.

The young females were called pullets. Once the range pullets began laying eggs, we moved them into the chicken houses. Pullet eggs were small, about half the size of a regular chicken egg. We called them pee-wees. They had no commercial value and were usually discarded. Sometimes we had them soft-boiled for breakfast but mostly we just played with them. When I could get away with it, I liked throwing them against the barn wall and watching their gooey contents oozing down.

"Damn it," Dad would yell, "Stop that." And that would be the last of it, at least, for that day.

At the end of the summer the now mature hens were moved into the chicken coops. The summer shelters were moved to an alternate range. The summer's manure was left behind to be composted and percolate into the earth. We had a front range that butted up on the Richard Road south of our house. The back range was adjacent to the woods in back of the farm.

If there was one job on the farm that I disliked, it was helping to vaccinate the pullets against the paramyxovirus that caused Newcastle disease—a fatal illness in chickens. This was done in mid-summer when they were still on the range.

The vaccinations always meant a long half-day that began before dawn. The round-up the night before was fun. Most of the pullets preferred to sleep in their range shelters at night. A few liked to wander about while others managed to fly high enough to sit on the enclosing fence or fly to the outside—then they would wander along the edge hoping to find a way back in. The object of the evening was to get them all into the shelters and fasten the wire doors shut.

Frank and I had a routine for catching the stragglers. I imagined it was like a cattle drive, directing them toward the fence, one at a time. Then Frank would come from one side and I from the other—one of us would grab the bird. Holding the chicken by the legs, her head hanging down, the way chickens are always carried, we proclaimed victory.

As we headed to the gate to get back into the range, Frank, carrying the now calm pullet, asked, "I wonder why they don't fight us when we carry them by the legs?"

"Maybe their brains stop working when they're upside-down," I answered.

Once inside, Frank would carry the chicken to the nearest shelter as I unlatched the gate, then he would let the white fluffy bird flop in. That was the good part of the job.

The next day began early, with the sunrise. Dad would wait with bottles of vaccine while the rest of us got organized. Frank or I would stand hunched over in the shelter grabbing the chickens by the legs. Three chickens held in one hand were passed to the one standing just outside the shelter door. He, in turn, handed one chicken at a time to Mom. Still holding the chicken by the legs, she spread out one wing. Dad would dip a needle attached to a wooden holder into the vaccine bottle, then stab it through the outstretched wing. Mom would then release the squawking chicken and the process was quickly repeated—1,200 times, 1,200 birds.

Occasionally, Mom would drop one before Dad had a chance to stab the wing. That resulted in immediate recriminations by Dad. "Damn it, you weren't paying attention," he would yell.

It was one of those rare times that Dad shouted at Mom and she accepted the admonishment with her head bowed, like a whipped cat. Those moments were brief since one of us was already handing her the next chicken and Dad was hastily extending the pin back into the vaccine bottle.

None of us knew about herd immunity—the few non-immunized chickens were still protected since the virus couldn't spread when so many of the others were immune. Both Mom and Dad always sought perfection and missing an occasional pullet was unacceptable to both. After three hours we would break for a quick snack—a glass of milk and a cookie—and then we were back in the field again.

After several years, there was another reason for the three hour break. "Mom," I wheezed, the first time it happened, "I can't breathe anymore."

I was inside the shelter grabbing the pullets and handing them to Frank outside. Mom looked at me and announced, "Let's take a rest."

When we went back to finish, Mom revised the order. Now she worked inside the shelter while I held the pullet and stretched out the wing for Dad. That evening we went to Freehold where Dr. Lewis, our family doctor, pronounced that I had asthma caused by an allergy to chicken feathers.

That changed the impromptu field assembly line. Frank had the permanent position of working inside the shelter while I worked outside the door. When that caused an attack of asthma, Mom and I traded places. I now became the recipient of Dad's infrequent, "Damn it, you're not paying attention," outbursts. Mom would smile but never say a word.

By noon, the entire flock was immunized. We'd clean up and Mom would serve us our favorite foods—mine was a pumpernickel sandwich with big chunks of spicy salami. She would beam at Frank and me as if we had performed a heroic mission. For us, it was a moment of victory. After a vaccination session, Frank and I could do no wrong. At least, for a while.

The pullets—now grown into mature hens—were moved from the range to the chickenhouses at the end of the summer. There they would not spend energy searching out grass and insects to eat, chasing after one another, or trying to fly up to sit on top of the shelters or the fence.

In the chicken coops, the focus was on the business at hand—eating and laying eggs.

The houses for the laying chickens were a series of long buildings divided into rooms. Each would hold 150 female chickens. Every room had two feed hoppers, raised eighteen inches from the floor. They were long metal containers with attached footboards for the chickens to stand on and were filled with a mix of wheat and corn. Nearby was an automatic water fountain, and, on the two sidewalls, a series of metal nests, layered with straw, where the hens nested and laid their eggs. The back of the room held a long wooden nighttime roost, wired to the ceiling. A manure pit was built underneath this roosting area. A couple of men from the Bridgewater farm shoveled out the pits every few months, carting the manure back to their farm for fertilizer.

The chickens, having no teeth, swallowed the hard corn kernels and dried wheat seeds whole. A small metal container of finely crushed oyster shells hung on one wall. After feeding on the grain, the chickens would gobble up the sharp bits of hard shells. These lodged in their crop—a sack in their gullet that the feed passed through—and ground up the corn and wheat they ate.

There was no individuality to any of our hens. They had a flock personality. Their major interest was in eating and they would line up in great anticipation at feeding time. They had learned it on the range as pullets and still did it as hens. Clucking away, they seemed to be gossiping with one another about the event to come.

They also knew how to find the nest to lay their eggs, an event that occurred almost daily. They were easily frightened, especially when we approached the chicken coop and surprised them. The room would suddenly erupt into a frenzy of flying hens and a cloud of dust and white feathers. The risk of a chicken injuring itself was significant. It became automatic for us to approach the chicken houses with the loud announcement of, "heads high, heads high."

If the birds knew you were coming, they would get a bit agitated and make a high pitched clucking noise in their throats. This would soon give way to a brooding sound, a quick and gentle "buck, buck, buck," in a low and comforting tone. It said, "Come on—we're okay."

Chickens are omnivorous creatures. If they see a speck of blood, the whole flock will attack the injured bird. If there is a little blood on the chicken after laying an especially large egg, the attack is on. The assault can be so severe, that intestines might be seen hanging from the injured rectum.

To combat this destructive behavior, each chicken was fitted with a pair of solid metal discs, looking like a pair of opaque glasses. These little specks were held in place by tiny cotter pins inserted through the top of the beak, preventing the bird from seeing straight ahead. This was done at the time they were moved from the range into their permanent chicken coops. The specks gave them a scholarly look that belied their small, simple brains.

We used the same process as for the vaccinations. As we put them in the cages for transport, Dad fitted each one with a set of metal specs, deftly pushing a tiny cotter pin through the holes in the specs and the top of the beak. These miniature solid metal "glasses" kept the chickens from seeing straight ahead but did not impede their ability to eat or drink or finding their way around—sort of the opposite of blinders on a horse. Somehow, however, it stopped them from seeing a cut or bleeding area on a fellow chicken which would cause them to attack and kill that bird. Strangely, the specs never seemed to bother the hens, the beak was made of a fingernail-like substance and must not have had much feeling. Applying them was finished in one swift movement but it had to be done carefully and so was laborious and took till mid-afternoon.

We stopped the insertion of the specs after several years. Instead, Dad began using a red tarry paste to cover any exposed lesions that might provoke an attack or cannibalization.

"That stuff smells awful," I said.

"That's the point," Dad responded. "The chickens don't like it either. They won't get near a wound that's smeared with it."

"I hope the smell comes off your hands better than when you got gassed killing that skunk last year," I said. He had caught the skunk in one of the chicken coops looking for eggs. Mom made him undress outside and he must have spent an hour in the shower.

Dad just looked at me, not smiling.

Not using the specs seemed much more humane to me. It certainly made the late summer chore less onerous.

As a small boy, I wanted a chicken for a pet. I liked the soft touch of the silky white feathers and the contrasting bright red color of their flopped-over combs. Chickens might not be intelligent, but they were smart enough to be wary of people. They would never let me get near them except under one circumstance—when they were in one of the nests busy laying an egg. At those moments they were entirely absorbed in the act of getting the egg laid.

One of my chores was collecting eggs into a wire basket—carefully lifting them out of the unoccupied nests when the chickens were feeding, and gently placing them in the basket to avoid cracking them. If I encountered a chicken in the process of laying, I always stopped to run my hand over their smooth white feathers, imaging they enjoyed it as much as my dog liked being petted. Sometimes I would press on the bird's abdomen, helping it push the egg out. I liked catching the warm moist white egg. I was like an obstetrician delivering a baby.

My asthma attacks became more frequent as the years went by. Going into the chicken coops to collect the eggs brought on wheezing episodes. The asthma contributed to my frequent colds. By the time I was ready for high school, Dad decided he would have a hired hand help with the farm chores instead of me. I didn't like the asthma but as it turned out, it wasn't all bad either. Miraculously, there were no more attacks. I seemed to have finally outgrown it and just in time to begin my high school track career.

There were no roosters in among the hens during most of the year. They had long ago been culled out as baby chicks by Henry Rapp's men. The occasional rooster that got through and made the mistake of announcing his presence with the familiar morning call of "cock-a-doo-dle-do" never made it off the range, usually ending up in Mom's chicken pot. Contrary to the common belief that the presence of males inspired the hens, roosters were really a distraction and reduced the egg production. And in those days, no one ate fertile eggs. Health food stores that touted the supposed value and flavor of fertile eggs didn't become popular until the 1970s.

There was one exception to the "no roosters" rule. In early spring, Henry and his men would bring a truckload of roosters and distribute them into the chicken coops that housed the one-year-old hens. This was the time of year that Henry would buy fertilized eggs from Dad. Henry and Dad had a special relationship. Henry liked Dad's careful and orderly way of farming. He especially liked the meticulous way he cared for his hens and his always conscientious, on-time vaccination program. We were the only ones Henry used in the breeding process—other than those from his own large farm.

The arrival of the roosters would really stir up activity and create considerable excitement, both for the hens and me. The fertilized eggs went back to the hatchery where they were artificially incubated for the spring sale of baby chicks in warm boxes with light bulbs to keep the temperature even. Hens were not needed to sit on the eggs—light bulbs would do. Henry paid a premium price for the fertilized eggs and that always proved to be a windfall for us.

I was intrigued by the fertilization process. A rooster would surprise a hen or chase her until she stopped. She would bend her knees and spread her wings ever so slightly while he jumped on her back. Then, grabbing the back of her neck with his beak, he would carry out a burst of rhythmic motions with his pelvis. As quickly as it began, it was over. In between eating and sleeping, the roosters were at it all day. After a few weeks, Henry retrieved the roosters and the chicken house was quiet— the drama was over.

During one of these springs, I must have been ten or eleven, Mom was trying to gently introduce me to the subject of sexuality. One evening, when she was having me read about the birds and the bees, I asked her, "Does Dad bite your neck at night in bed?"

"Why don't you put the book away," she said. "I think you understand more than you should."

THE OUTHOUSE

THE KNOCK on the back door was soft and hesitant.

"Mom, there's…" I began, looking up from my homework but Mom was already on her way. I put the papers I was using into my spelling book. It was always special when someone came to visit—a new event to savor and an excuse to stop schoolwork for a while.

The man standing in the open doorway wore blue overalls and a patched plaid shirt, his hair was disheveled and his face browned by years of work in the sun. He was the new handyman that Dad had recently hired.

"Mrs. Gutmann, I need to ask you for a favor," he said looking down at his shoes.

"Is everything alright, Mr. Mitchell?" Mom asked; her crisp German accent in sharp contrast to his easy New Jersey drawl.

"Yes, ma'am," he answered. "I got one of the two chicken roosts all fixed up nice and I'm ready to start the last one. I should have it fixed by lunch time."

Mom hesitated while he paused.

"Ma'am, I need to borrow the rest room," he said, still looking down at his feet.

She smiled at him and asked, "The rest room?" her voice was laced with uncertainty.

"Yes, ma'am," he said. "The bathroom . . ."

"Oh, you mean the toilet," Mom said, her face lighting up with sudden comprehension. "There's an outside one in front of the big chickenhouse. It's little hard to see."

"Thank you, ma'am," he said, "I'll find it." He backed down off the porch.

Mom came back into the kitchen. She stood at the counter mixing onions and spices into raw hamburger in a large bowl.

"Can you believe it," she said, full of astonishment, "He calls the toilet the rest room."

"The kids in school call it that, too," I said.

"I can't imagine someone going to the toilet to rest," Mon answered. "It's a place to do your business. Only in America would someone call it a rest room." Another thought occurred to Mom. "And he wanted to borrow it," she added. "What a funny expression."

I had wondered about the strange small closet-like structure in front of the big chickenhouse. No one ever paid attention to it nor was it talked about—as if it didn't exist—and it was never used for anything as far as I could tell. All our buildings were carefully painted white but this one was ignored, the cedar boards all weathered and gray. The tar paper roof was frayed with age. A wooden latch was used to keep the door closed. Inside there was a large boxy structure standing on the dirt floor with a hole in its center. I couldn't see anything looking down the dark opening but the shroud of cobwebs filling the tiny room motivated me to leave quickly. It had been a place of mystery.

I thought about our two bathrooms with their tile floors and shower stalls and white porcelain toilets. The outside toilet seemed awful.

"Why didn't you let him use the downstairs bathroom?" I asked.

"He's very polite and a good worker but we don't know him very well," she answered. "You have to be careful who you let in the house."

"But you don't make Mr. Herzberg go outside," I said.

Mr. Herzberg came to visit us every few months on his motor scooter. He worked as a farm hand for Otto Goldstein whose chicken farm was a few miles away. Mr. Goldstein had been a federal judge in Germany before immigrating and had managed to bring Mr. Herzberg with him. His visits gave me the opportunity to admire the scooter.

"Doesn't use much gas," he would proudly explain. He always wore dark pants and a black leather jacket, even in the summer time.

Mostly, he came to gossip with Mom. Dad didn't spend any time with him.

"He doesn't have anything useful to say," Dad told me. "Besides, he's not very smart."

I'd hang around, anyway. It was all about the gossip and the scooter.

"So, how come he gets to go to the bathroom in the house?" I asked.

"He's a Jewish refugee, like we are," she explained.

I must have had a puzzled expression on my face. "We have to take care of our own," she added. "No one else will."

"But, Mom," I said. I was back to thinking about the outside toilet, "it's full of cobwebs and spiders."

I had visions of those tiny creatures crawling all over me and biting. And then there was the hole. I'd be afraid to sit on it, I thought. I could get splinters in my bottom and worse—fall through the hole. The idea of falling in was frightening. The hole looked to be pretty deep.

Mom had finished mixing the hamburger and was now making patties. The two cats, sitting on the window sill outside, looked hungrily through the window screen at her. I'd watched the process many times before. She would wrap the hamburgers in wax paper and put them in the refrigerator.

"You know, there's no toilet paper out there," I said.

"You're right. I didn't think about it," she answered. She paused, and then asked, "Would you like a bit hamburger?"

She had made a ball of meat, about the size of a large marble, and held it out in her hand. I loved the taste of raw hamburger, onions, and spices. She walked over and dropped it on my tongue, like a mother bird feeding her young. I knew what was coming next—it always did.

"You know, in France this is a great delicacy," she said.

"Yes, you've told me, beef tartar."

She smiled and kissed my cheek.

"Is Mr. Mitchell poor?" I asked.

"Yes, he is," she answered. "He is such a good handyman but he drinks too much. He's often drunk and then he can't work. He has a wife and three children. I feel sorry for them."

"Can't we help them?" I asked.

"I don't think we can do more than what we do," Mom answered. "Your father pays him well. Alcoholism is a terrible problem."

I didn't understand. "What's alcoholism?" I asked.

"It's when people drink too much wine and whiskey or schnapps and cognac," Mom answered. "Too much alcohol makes people sick and they can't work."

"You and Dad drink wine sometimes," I said, "and Dad has a Hennessey once in a while when something good happens."

"A little makes you feel happy," she said, "but some people drink too much—like Mr. Mitchell. It's a terrible thing."

I remembered some of the boys at school talking about bars. "Is the Blue Moon where people drink schnapps?" I asked.

"Yes," she answered, "but I think it's mostly beer and whiskey."

I smiled to myself. My question about the Blue Moon was finally solved. Suddenly, I remembered something else the boys had been talking about at school. Outhouses. Now I knew the name of our primitive outside toilet.

"Mom," I asked. "Do you know what they use for toilet paper in an outhouse?"

She was putting the wrapped patties into the refrigerator. The cats watched her every move. "Outhouse," she hesitated for a moment, "So, that's what it's called."

"They use a Sears' catalogue," I said. "People tear pages out of it."

Mom looked over at me and shook her head. "Borrowing rest rooms and now Sears' catalogues hanging in outhouses. How do the Americans come up with these ideas?"

THE RELATIVES

THE VISITS from our New York City relatives were always important events. They were special for different reasons.

Aunt Sarah and Uncle Gustav arrived in their big black Cadillac driven in state by a chauffeur. I had seen the Queen and King of England in the movie newsreels and I always thought that Sarah and Gustav Lowenthal were the queen and king of New York City—at least, that was the impression Mom gave me.

Before each visit Mom would remind me that it was her Aunt Sarah who gave us the affidavit that allowed us to come to the United States and escape the brutalities of the Nazi regime. Each time it was said as if it were a revelation—not that I hadn't heard it a dozen times before.

Aunt Sarah would always say, "Gustav, just look at those two boys of Rosa's. They are so well behaved, just as boys should be." (Uncle Gustav had changed his name in America to Edward, but Aunt Sarah still called him by his original name.)

Mom always smiled and then patted me on the head. I would look up at her, for a moment thinking she believed the compliment. The Lowenthals would come in time for afternoon coffee and it was always a splendid affair. The dining room table would be set with Mom's best Bavarian china and freshly-picked flowers in a crystal vase at the center of the table. The delicate coffee cups, with fragile handles all pointing to the right, were planted in their saucers, each standing at quiet attention like the Coldstream guards of her Majesty's regiment of sentries.

"Don't touch the cups," Mom would remind me. "They are very delicate and break easily."

Mom should know, I thought but didn't say, she'd broken one herself when she washed them after the last visit. She'd spent hours trying to glue the handle back but she finally threw it out after Dad pronounced her efforts as unsatisfactory.

The day of the visit, while Dad was occupied caring for the chickens and collecting eggs, Mom started her baking early in the morning. The warm aroma of her pastries filled the house. My favorite was the crumb cake (Streuselkuchen) but the fruit pies were almost as good. The swirling patterns of the marble cake (Marmorkuchen) with its sprinkled coat of white powdery sugar were fun to look at but the cake was too dry for my taste. Schneckennudels were my all-time favorite. They were made of rolled yeast dough, and filled with sweet raisins and cinnamon, but they were far too gooey for genteel company. They would have to wait for another day.

Aunt Sarah always presented me with a shiny silver dollar. Like the coins in my coin collection, these were much too imposing to spend. Silver dollars were special.

"Now you know why Aunt Sarah is such a rich woman," Mom would tell me after every visit, "She could have brought you a book or a toy but she is not generous with gifts." It was meant as criticism but the touch of admiration and gratitude for the old lady was still there in Mom's voice.

When other relatives came to visit, they would travel by bus from New York. The bus would stop at a gas station on Highway 9, a few miles away. Dad was always there to pick them up in our blue Chevy. There were my mother's cousins, a step-brother and step-sister and their families. Mom's dad (Opa to us), would stay a few weeks every year, living in his special room on the first floor where the sausages usually hung to cure and dry, and where clean laundry was stored.

My two favorite relatives were both uncles: Dad's brother, Ben, and Mom's brother, Friedl. Ben was my American uncle who told funny stories and taught me how to play baseball. Friedl was the most fun. He was always full of mischief and always in trouble with his younger sister.

"It's like having Max and Moritz in the house," she would say, with a mixture of annoyance and amusement.

I could easily associate either of the two cartoon characters with Friedl, and I liked him for his humor. Friedl would usually arrive at bedtime, no matter what time he was expected. A life in farming meant long, tiring days for Mom and Dad but that didn't seem to matter to Friedl, he expected dinner, no matter the time. His excuse was always the same; that his sales trips to millinery shops in various New Jersey towns took longer than he thought. This was probably true, but it was still annoying. The back seat of his car was covered with women's hats, veils, and artificial flowers (Mom called them fake flowers) which he sold to millinery shops throughout New Jersey.

I would lie in bed upstairs listening to Friedl and Mom argue about his late arrival. He'd changed his real name, Siegfried, to Sidney when he arrived in America but no one in the family called him anything but Friedl. He changed his last name, too—from Kahn to Kane—so he would be American despite his German-French accent.

Friedl was shaped just like Dad, short and stocky, and he was bald like Dad. In fact, all the men in Mom and Dad's families were bald. Friedl had a small square moustache that gave him a Charlie Chaplin look and he was just as funny. He had a never-ending supply of jokes.

"Why does a good wurst sandwich taste like the ocean?"

"Uncle Friedl, that joke has a three foot long beard," I would answer, laughing. The long beard was another of his jokes. "You've told it a hundred times."

"But do you remember the answer?" he would ask.

"*Mehr, Meer,*" I was still laughing. They were German homonyms, the first meaning more and the second, ocean.

"Yes," he grinned. "It tastes like the ocean."

Then, after making certain that the joke had a satisfactory impact, Friedl added, "And remember this important piece of wisdom." He was already laughing. He loved food jokes.

"'When things are tough,' the poor man said,
'I eat my wurst without the bread.'"

Mom was smiling, working at the kitchen sink. Friedl was being Friedl. His joking was interrupted by the sound of Dad scraping manure from his shoes outside by the back porch. When he walked in, Friedl was suddenly serious and said to Dad, "You remember Leo Goldberg?" Dad nodded his head. "I heard that the Nazi's arrested him and put him in a concentration camp. His brother lives near me in the city. It's a terrible thing."

That got Mom started on her all-time favorite subject. She was no longer smiling, her face and voice full of indignation. "Those damned Germans are just an evil lot. Mr. Goldberg lost his leg in the first war. He was a German hero then. Nobody cared about his religion then. And now? Now he is a Jew and not a real German. They will kill him. Nobody cares that he almost died defending his fatherland. Look at Friedl with his hand injury and Sally who still has a scar on his forehead where he was shot. They were Germans when they needed soldiers and now they are Jews when they need scapegoats. Phooey."

Friedl had been injured in the First World War when the machine gun he was firing exploded. I'd never seen anyone with a misshapen hand before. Living with missing fingers seemed impossible but Friedl managed to turn it to his advantage at least once. This was the time he'd been in a private club in New York City watching the gambling. At least, he said he was only an observer. But when the police barged in, he was arrested along with everyone else. At his court hearing, the officer said Friedl was gambling at the poker table. Friedl denied it.

"When you arrested him," Friedl's lawyer asked the officer, "did you notice anything unusual about Mr. Kane?"

"No, sir," he answered,

"Was there anything different about his hands?"

"No."

Turning to Friedl, he said, "Mr. Kane, would you hold up your hands for the court to see."

Friedl held them up. His left hand had three fingers missing. Only the index and little fingers were present. The right hand had no index finger. He couldn't have been playing cards with those hands. The judge dismissed the case. It made a good story.

Mom really liked Friedl. Her oldest brother, Ernst, treated her as an older brother might—full of advice and always with what, he believed, was the right answer. Friedl was her fun-loving brother who could always make her laugh.

Ernst had escaped with his family to Palestine and he did so at the last moment before the war. By that time, the Nazis didn't allow those emigrating to take anything much with them, but he managed. Ernst did not share Dad's fear of authority. Mom always said Ernst was full of courage and daring. He saw spiriting assets out of Germany as a challenge and arranged the smuggling of small amounts of gold for my father as well. There were whispers of people who had swallowed small pieces of gold or who hid small bars or coins among their belongings or in their cars just before crossing the border into Switzerland.

"The man has nerves of steel," Mom said, referring to Ernst, "he went to Palestine with diamonds stuffed up his rectum."

"In his rectum?" I was incredulously. "That's dangerous. You told me never to put anything up my bottom." I remembered an admonishment some time earlier.

"And somehow he got gold out, too," she added.

"Gold in his rectum with the diamonds?" I had a vision of a piece of chicken intestine stuffed with diamonds and gold coins. "How could he even walk? That had to hurt a lot."

"I don't know how he smuggled the gold," she said, ignoring my concerns.

Mom claimed Ernst took too big a share of the smuggled gold for himself. Dad never talked about it but Mom was full of anger and when she was angry, she talked about her feelings and her suspicions. When we left, in 1937, the laws that affected refugees were just being enacted. It was still possible to evade them, if you knew how—but it meant taking awful chances.

Uncle Ben came often. "But I like Uncle Ben," I would say, knowing Mom was critical of him—critical, as she so often said, that he had not done enough to try saving Julius, Rosel, the three girls, and Oma. Still, he was a favorite uncle. He taught me how to play baseball and always brought toys when he visited the farm on a long weekend. He took me to my first baseball game at Yankee Stadium and showed me how to use a scorecard. He knew all the players and their stats. By contrast, my father thought it was all a waste of time and unimportant, especially, since he didn't understand the game—it was strictly an American sport—and he didn't have time for it.

Mom would never respond to my defense of Uncle Ben—her anger with him had deeper roots. In spite of her feelings, she kept welcoming both him and Aunt Clara to the farm. They were relatives, after all.

"Ben was the playboy of the family," my mother would say. My grandfather had done odd jobs and occasionally sold cattle in the small German village of Moenshrot, and the family was poor. Dad, after getting out of the German Army, was determined to get ahead in business. Ben chose a different path to escape the family's poverty and came to the United States in the 1920s. Did he emigrate to escape a forced marriage? That was a rumor, never substantiated. His great success was selling insurance.

Ben was one of my boyhood heroes. He filled a role my Dad had no time to serve. He was a trim man with graying curly hair and a perpetual smile. He never seemed serious like Dad. The relationship with Ben must have been very complex for my parents. He was, after all, Dad's brother and had helped us after we arrived in New York—he had lots of useful advice about jobs and life in America. I remember our living with them when we first arrived and, later, frequent visits to their apartment. Dad never said how he felt about Ben but they always seemed to get along. Mom's anger was tempered by her sense of family and by Ben's helpfulness and goodwill.

In 1993, when Ben was in his nineties, we had lunch at the World Trade Center. "Mom always had mixed feelings about you," I said, trying to be tactful but wanting to know. Mom and Dad had died some time before.

"I know," he said. He knew exactly where I was heading. "And I always felt bad about it. I think the truth was just too hard for your mother to bear. I had written Julius, I don't know how many times, about coming to America and bringing my sister and the girls." Ben's strong New York accent was still tinged with a touch of German. "Julius was unwilling to give up his career until it was too late. He was sure that the Nazi movement could not survive in a country with such a strong cultural tradition. Even Aunt Rosel couldn't change his mind. I went back once to visit just before war broke out to persuade them and it made no difference. Your grandmother felt she was too old. She said she'd take her chances. You know, she was supposed to have died in a home but who knows. I never did find out what happened to Rosel and her family, but, still, I know. We all know."

DEAD COUSINS

A MASSIVE BOOKCASE made of solid walnut dominated our formal front parlor. It had doors glazed in small panels and extended across one entire wall and almost to the ceiling. An imposing feather-stuffed couch and three oversized upholstered chairs sat together in serious company in the middle of the room. In spite of the grand furniture, however, the focus of the whole room was a framed photographer's portrait of three young girls—my three cousins. The picture stood for years on the glass covered walnut-veneer coffee table next to the fireplace in our farm parlor.

We boys were allowed in the parlor only to look at books our mother had brought from Germany, or, when we had company—neatly dressed and hair brushed—we were expected to sit and show our best behavior to the guests. Sitting on the heavily-upholstered arms of the couch was not tolerated but Mom allowed Dad to take his afternoon nap on the soft cushions. Clean hands and polished shoes were the rules in that room for everyone but most particularly for small boys.

We were sure my three young cousins (shown in the picture with their parents), as well as my dad's sister, Aunt Rosel, and her husband, Uncle Julius, had died in a concentration camp somewhere in Germany. My mother feared this would happen when we were still in Germany and begged them to emigrate but Julius was arrested just before we left.

"With Rosel gone, your father has only one sister left," Mom said. She was referring to Babette, who lived in New York City with her brother, Uncle Ben.

The three girls were revered by my mother. They looked out from the frame with gentle and serious and, it seemed to me, worried faces. That small picture was my Mother's shrine. To her, there seemed little doubt that their deaths and the death of my grandmother were a travesty and a testimony to German inhumanity—a reflection of the cruelty and brutality of the Germans. The girls became symbols to her of the enormous number of innocent lives lost because of hatred and prejudice. We knew this part of our family had all disappeared, but little of the circumstances or exactly when.

The last two times we heard from Julius and Rosel were in late 1940 and 1941—our first year on the farm. My parents' days were consumed by long hours of work and the news of ever-worsening German atrocities only added to their burden. Rumors of newer and larger concentration camps and Jews being murdered were spoken and written about constantly. The *Aufbau* was full of such news.

Ben forwarded a letter from Julius. He reported that Jetta, Dad's mother, had died December 3, 1940 in Lublin, Poland. She had been deported there and lived the last three months of her life in a nursing home or a psychiatric hospital. It wasn't clear which.

"The Nazi's probably tortured her to death," Mom said, her face cloaked in anger.

"Julius says she was confused and disoriented the entire time," Dad continued to read from the letter.

Why would anyone want to kill people? I could understand killing wild animals. Skunks smelled dreadful and killed chickens. The groundhogs dug holes and messed up the range. But people? I didn't understand. Mom said the Germans were evil and, for some reason I couldn't understand, they hated Jews. Why? None of it made any sense to me.

It was January 1941, when the last letter came from Julius. It had been forwarded several times and it wasn't clear where it was from. "Some of our friends have been taken to the camps. I was fortunate to find work harvesting the fall crops for a farmer and now we have some food for the winter. We still have heard nothing from the American consulate. They know we've been promised an affidavit and we have paid into a trust but still no news. And the Germans won't issue an exit visa for us. I've written Ben and hope he can talk with the consulate in New York to see if anything can be done."

"It will take a miracle to get Julius and Rosel and the girls out now," Mom said quietly. She looked as helpless as a little child facing an unseen terror. "If only they hadn't waited so long."

Dad just shook his head. He knew the worst would happen. After that day, every time she would dust the picture when I was with her she would announce, "An affidavit, that's all it would have taken, an affidavit, and they'd all be alive today."

"I thought you said they didn't want to leave Germany," I would say, but she would just ignore me. She wasn't expecting a discussion, she was teaching a gospel—a truth—to a small and argumentative audience of one.

Documents are sacred to those who are forced to flee. Besides proving nationality they can show that someone influential cares about you and may defend or help you in some way. The affidavit Mom talked about was a promise, a promise that guaranteed the family immigrating would not require government welfare. Our sponsor was my mother's wealthy aunt, who had also vouched for my Uncle Friedl and Opa. They had promised one for Julius and Rosel but somehow it was too late. There were other forces in play by the time they decided to leave.

"Your brother, Ben, could have saved them all," Mom would repeat her litany to Dad whenever the subject arose—actually she usually brought it up herself. "He's been in America God knows how many years? He could have arranged it all easily. And what did he tell everybody? 'Don't worry, this thing will blow over.' Well, it didn't and now they're dead—all three of those wonderful girls and their parents."

"Ben is not a responsible person and neither is his New York wife," my mother would declare, standing at the big sink in the kitchen, washing the dishes, dominating the scene. These diatribes usually came after she had finished dusting the living room and the martyred nieces were in her thoughts. "New York wife" was Mom's way of pegging Clara as a common woman.

"They should be ashamed. How can they hold their heads up, letting those three lovely girls and Ben's mother die in concentration camps when they had the means to help?"

Mom was obsessed. As I grew older I felt the full weight of her concerns—and this was only the first. There seemed endless conversations built around this theme. I was too young to understand the full dynamics then. I thought it was just the tragedy and sense of loss that kept Mom at it. I never thought that guilt might play a role— guilt that we had escaped and others hadn't—a common feeling in wartime. There was also a possibility, never mentioned, that Mom could have done more herself.

been converted into a church. The kids said in that school you had to go to the outhouse if you needed to use the toilet—even in the winter. I was glad it wasn't my school. Sometimes I wondered if our synagogue had once been a one-room schoolhouse even though Dad assured me that it hadn't.

The kids were all white. They had traditionally been all Christian as well, but that was slowly changing with the arrival of the Jewish farmers. There weren't any black students. It's not that they went to a segregated school as they did in nearby Freehold Junior and High Schools, there simply were no black families living in the rural parts of the township. They did not work on the chicken farms; they only came into the area in summer when fruit and vegetables were picked. In fall they went back down south again. I never saw any black kids until I went to high school.

Every day at school started off with the pledge of allegiance and a prayer. The pledge was good—I liked being an American—but the prayers often made me feel uneasy. I always breathed a secret sigh of relief when the teacher began with, "The Lord is my shepherd. . ." The 23rd psalm was from the Old Testament. Even the Lord's Prayer, "Our Father who art in heaven. . ." from the New Testament was fine. It was the mention of Jesus that made me feel as if I were an outsider—that I was different and did not belong.

My view of Christ was that he hated the Jews and had sent some of my classmates as his modern-day disciples to persecute and torment me. If Jesus was about, "Do unto others as you would have them do unto you," these disciples didn't know about it.

Their epithets were confusing and frightening. They went from: "Christ killer," to "Jews are no good at sports."

None of it made sense to me but it did fuel my anxiety

that I might not be good at sports. I soon discovered I could run fast. This ability was useful in escaping from them—quite often. It also came in handy later when I excelled at track. So much for Jews not being good at sports, but I didn't know that until high school.

The killing of Jesus was a major issue. I'd never killed anything bigger than a fly. Watching the shochet dispatching a chicken was difficult enough for me. The killing of a human being was beyond me. The Nazis were killing Jews in Germany and Poland and now I was being accused of killing Christ.

"Jesus died thousands of years ago," I would say, "how could I or my parents have anything to do with it?"

"Your ancestors did it," was the answer, "and you have to pay."

The deed simply needed avenging and I was there. My tormentors just laughed at my explanation and made their slurs more venomous.

When we sang, "Onward Christian soldiers, marching as to war..." in class, I thought, what a bloodthirsty bunch these Christians are. But then, again, the Jews of the Old Testament weren't much better. They were also all about war, killing the first born of the enemy, or stealing a brother's birthright. I remembered our reading in Sunday school about beating swords into plowshares. That seemed like the right thing to do but it didn't last long. And now we were at war with the Germans who wanted to kill all the Jews. The Christians were sure a mean bunch. Mom might be right after all.

Christ's self-appointed devotees were everywhere—in the school bus, the classroom, the boys' room, and the playground. Their taunts were always just out of earshot of the teachers. The girls would just watch the drama without participating. It was the boys who were chosen to be the avengers, not the girls.

The ministers from local churches provided invocations and closing prayers at every major school function. Without fail, the prayers invoked the name of Jesus Christ or the Father, the Son, and the Holy Ghost. For some reason there was never a Rabbi to give the blessing.

I felt bothered by the frequent references to Christ but I kept my frustration to myself. Later, I heard that some Jewish mothers complained to the principal. For a while, some of the ministers skipped the references to Jesus but then he slipped back in again.

The teachers were never showed any anti-Jewish bias. My opinion was, that all of Christ's modern day disciples were boys, was constantly reinforced—but the important people in my life, the teachers, were all women. And the girls copied the teachers.

There was plenty of other subtle racism in the classroom that I didn't understand until years later. All the great American heroes were Caucasian as well as Christian—Abraham Lincoln, George Washington, Colin Kelly, Nathan Hale and George Custer. Custer was idolized because of his stand against the Indians at Little Bighorn. The Indians—frequently called red-skins—were usually depicted in the westerns of the day as a villainous subhuman race of people. Since they wouldn't accept Christianity, they were labeled as heathen. I identified with the Indians—they were victims of the great Christian white majority just as I often was.

My first realization that Indians could be counted among the good guys came from the Lone Ranger. Our house was full of books—all in German. My first American book was Fran Striker's *Lone Ranger and Tonto*. It was a memorable eighth birthday gift. Tonto's close relationship with the Lone Ranger mattered to me. He had saved the injured Texas Ranger who would become the Lone Ranger—there could be no greater feat.

Slavery had ended long before my childhood but Negroes, as a group, (the term, African-American, was far in the future), still came off as slave-like in school. Like the Indians, they were depicted as inferior to white people. Stephen Foster's songs—Old Black Joe and the Camptown Races—were popular, portraying Negroes as kindly, simple people who were not like us.

The bigotry of the National Geographic magazine was much more subtle. It had great pictures and the teachers all recommended it. Mom agreed with the general opinion and we had a subscription for years. The magazine often featured the lives of primitive African tribes. Like the Indians, they were depicted as interesting subhuman species. Native women were regularly presented unclad from the waist up. For a young boy, it was an unintended introduction into human sexuality.

The teachers did talk about George Washington Carver and his pioneering work with peanuts but he came across as a major exception. He and Tonto became my private heroes.

I was disappointed that there were so few Jewish Americans for a child like me to revere. Of course there was Albert Einstein—he was Mom's hero—but he was not really an American in my mind. Not with his heavy accent and wild hair. Besides, a boy needs young heroes and Einstein was far too old. There was Benny Goodman; but modern swing was not on Mom's music agenda. The only good music was classical, so Goodman got left out.

The only real hero I knew of was Hank Greenberg, the great Jewish slugger of the Detroit Tigers. I was in awe the first time I learned that he wouldn't play baseball on Yom Kippur, at a time when the Tigers were in the midst of a pennant race. I'm not sure I would have done that—except Mom would have insisted on it. Maybe he had a mom like mine.

THE YELLOW SCHOOL BUS

THE YELLOW BUS waited at the foot of our driveway. I ran out to get on board. Climbing up the three steep metal steps, I turned back to see my mother standing at the side of our house, her hands placed firmly on her narrow hips. She was shaking her head. I could almost hear her muttering to herself in her heavy German accent, "This is just a never-ending battle every morning—getting him to the bus on time." I turned back toward Mrs. Applegate who sat solidly planted in her large black leather seat, one hand on the steering wheel and the other on the crank handle, ready to shut the door.

"Good morning," I said, short of breath.

She looked at me, unsmiling and totally non-committal, unlike my mother standing in the yard, still shaking her head.

I took the empty double seat near the front and put my lunch box, with its picture of the Lone Ranger, beside me. I held my two schoolbooks and my homework clasped in my lap.

"Hey, Guts," a harsh voice in a stage whisper came from a few seats back, "kill any chickens today?"

I was glad I didn't have my violin case. That always created a new round of harassment. None of the other kids on our bus ever had to bring instruments to school.

"What's in the black case?" the harsh voice had asked accusingly two days before. "A tommy gun? Nah, I bet it's a squeak box." I hated my violin being called a squeak box. I hated having to take it to school. I wished the school didn't have an orchestra.

I hated it when the morning started out this way. Two girls giggled. The other kids didn't seem to pay attention. "Hey, I'm talking to you. Ain't you gonna' answer me?"

"Ain't" is not a word, I thought, but I didn't say anything. I clutched my books tighter and pulled the lunch box closer.

Suddenly he was sitting in the empty seat across the aisle. "No moving to another seat when I'm driving this bus," Mrs. Applegate announced. She was watching us in the rearview mirror. Bob flashed a big smile at her.

He leaned halfway across the aisle, looking straight at me. I kept my eyes fixed on the mirror. Mrs. Applegate wasn't looking—she seemed to have lost interest.

Bob kept staring at me. He wasn't much bigger than me except for his enormous head. His long, straight sandy hair was neatly parted and carefully plastered down. "Hey, I asked you a question. You been eatin' those chicken guts?"

Why was he after me?

Because I was the only Jewish boy on the bus?

Because I had parents who spoke with a funny accent?

Because I had to wear glasses?

Because I was no good at baseball?

Or maybe because I was carrying a violin case to school once every week?

Even a ten year-old could figure that out.

"Why don't you leave me alone; I'm not bothering you, am I?"

"Hey Chicken Guts, you're just a crybaby."

Bob was leaning all the way across the aisle now. I moved closer to the window to get away from him. He quickly jumped across the aisle and sat down next to me. I couldn't see Mrs. Applegate's eyes in the mirror—she was watching a girl who was getting on the bus.

Mom had told me to stay away from Bob. Now he was sitting next to me. I clutched my books and lunch box as tight as I could and squeezed myself flat against the side of the bus. My breath began to fog up the window.

"His father doesn't like our kind," my mother had told me. "He doesn't like Jews. Sometimes I think this is like Germany again."

"Hey, Guts, how come you always bring that lunch box? 'Cuz they don't serve food in the cafeteria that's blessed by a rabbi?" With his slicked up blond hair, I had visions he looked like a Nazi.

I really did want to buy lunch in the cafeteria but Mom said it was too expensive and, as Bob guessed, the meat wasn't kosher. Not that I cared. "Why don't you move back to the other seat and leave me alone," I said. This time I pushed his arm.

"Hey, Guts, I guess you wanna' fight? You hit me," he announced loudly as he pushed me hard. Looking up at the mirror, I could see Mrs. Applegate's eyes focus on us.

I pushed his face away from me—and I pushed harder than I thought. A trickle of blood came out of his nose and ran down his upper lip. You could hardly see it but I was suddenly proud. It was the first time I'd had the courage to defend myself and not run away as I usually did. In the mirror, Mrs. Applegate's gaze was focused right at me.

"We're almost there," she said. "You," she'd turned around as the bus stopped and now she was looking straight at me, "you and I are going directly to the principal's office."

Bob gave me a victorious smile. Why me, I thought? I didn't start the fight. Doesn't she know that? I felt like the whole world was picking on me.

My father arrived an hour later. He still wore work clothes under his black leather jacket. I was sure the call to pick me up had come while he was working in the chicken coops. He'd traded his white feed cap for a gray felt fedora. Mom had seen to that. He bowed gently toward Mrs. Griebling as he entered the office—it was his polite European custom. He held his hat in his hand and made no eye contact with the principal. He never did when there was trouble. I knew he would not stand up for me. He was fearful of people in authority. We were back in Nazi Germany again.

Dad turned to me with no expression on his face while Mrs. Griebling recited some of the events that had happened on the bus—at least the part where I bloodied Bob's nose, but not much of the run up to it.

"I'm so sorry that Ludwig caused you so much trouble. I promise it won't happen again."

Dad never said a word on the ten-minute ride home. I knew he was saving the harangue for Mom. He disliked any conflict and always avoided it, even with his sons. I also knew he felt shamed by my behavior.

As I got out of the car, he said, "Try not to get in a fight with your mother. Just listen to what she has to say. Don't get her upset."

Mom stood at the kitchen sink, just beginning to dry the breakfast dishes. She looked sternly at me as I walked in. She wore a shapeless housedress she'd made from cotton feed bags that had a white and pale blue print.

"Who was it?" she asked. I told her it was Bob.

She stopped and looked at me. For moment I thought she might smile but she kept her serious expression.

"That boy is no good," she said, now looking at Dad,

"and neither is his father. They're full of prejudice."

"Mom," I said, "I really didn't start the fight. Bob was pestering me on the bus. I was just trying to defend myself. I don't know why Mrs. Applegate thought I was the troublemaker."

I thought I heard her mumble, "She's just as bigoted as Bob's father and I'll bet she's his friend, on top of it all."

"Go upstairs to your room," she said to me, "and get out of those school clothes."

As I made my escape, she added, "When you're done, you can come back down for a glass of chocolate milk and a piece of cake." I looked back—she was smiling.

The School Principal

I WAS ALWAYS FEARFUL of Mrs. Griebling. Principals are the ultimate authority figures and, to young boys, the ultimate enemy. Teachers wielded authority, too, but tempered with an element of kindness and an interest in the student's progress. Not so with the principal. Her role was to scold and punish boys when they misbehaved. Being called to her office amounted to being summoned to the gates of hell—even at eleven, I imagined it a dark dungeon with walls lined with whips and cudgels.

Once, when there was some confusion in class about the spelling of principal—principle or principal—she had told us, "the clue is that the principal is your pal."

Not likely, I thought. Still, it was a good way to remember the spelling.

Mrs. Griebling was always there in the background as a force. She made the announcements that came across the PA system. You couldn't see her; you'd just hear her disembodied voice coming from a small box on the front classroom wall. There would be a crackling, static-y sound and then she would come on: "There will be a school assembly at eleven o'clock," she would declare in a deep and gravelly tone. The message was benign but she sounded as mean as we were sure she must be.

I had no contact with Mrs. Griebling in my early grades—but more than enough during the later ones. She was a heavyset, elderly, serious woman. I don't think she ever smiled—at least, not at me. Many of us thought she couldn't. A worried look seemed indelibly imprinted on her furrowed face. She appeared resigned to having a string of guilty boys parade through her office for various infractions. We were always guilty, of course.

Her skin was old and wrinkled. She wore her gray hair in a tight bun at the back of her head and it looked exactly the same every day. Some of us wondered if it was a wig. She wore a black shapeless dress with a nondescript white pattern that hung full length, down to her ankles. The dress seemed to be her only one.

When she raised her voice I imagined an irritated dog growling. She radiated an aura of toughness and meanness.

As I think back, I'm sure she made only a small salary even with her high position in our little community and she was probably afraid of little boys' energy and mischief, afraid of not doing her job to the parents' 1950s standards, maybe even afraid of getting fired, who knows?

Little boys in her school didn't see her point of view, we were just scared of her and the most awesome and feared event imaginable was to be sent to her office. She always sat behind her immense, dark mahogany desk, papers neatly placed in small stacks. An imposing grandfather clock stood to one side. I had to visit her there quite a few times and, each time, with a sense of foreboding and doom.

The fight with Bob in the school bus was not the first visit but it was the only one Mom and Dad knew about. The year before, I had been sent to her office for talking too much in class. The secretary opened the door and pointed to a chair. Gribbie—that's what we called her in the halls and on the playground—kept reading and signing letters as if I wasn't there.

I moved my head carefully so she wouldn't notice I was looking around the room. There were no heavy leather belts and bludgeons hanging on the walls. Maybe she hasn't brought them out yet, I thought. But there are no hooks to hang them on either, I realized. For a moment I relaxed. I might not get flogged after all.

The whole idea of being whipped frightened me. I had read about whipping and flogging in story books but had only heard about it in reality from one of the Garfinkles. They were one of our closest neighbors—and they were a strange family. Old man Garfinkle would drive his beat-up pick-up truck down Richard Road, his eyes glued straight ahead, never acknowledging those he passed. Their house and farm building were all in poor repair and their yard littered with discarded tires and farm equipment, broken crockery, and a wrecked car on blocks. Mom said it was disgusting the way they lived.

Their youngest son had cerebral palsy and he would occasionally come over to visit. When he looked at me, one of his eyes looked off in a different direction. His clothes were always dirty and his hair unkempt. One day he showed me red swollen welts on his back.

"How did you get them?" I'd asked.

"I got whacked with a belt." David answered. "My father does it when he gets mad at me."

I'd gotten spanked on my bottom in the past but the idea of using a belt was terrifying. I told Mom about it. She said it was a terrible thing to do to a child. Being whipped was my worse nightmare.

Finally, Gribbie looked up from her desk, straight at me. I could see she did have an evil eye, just as everyone told me she did.

"Ludwig," she began, it came out "Luud-wig," with a

long emphasis on the letter *u*, "your mother and father are hard-working people and they are trying to set a good example for you. You need to stop your foolishness in the classroom and pay attention to your work and to the teacher." She paused. "Do you understand?"

"Yes, ma'am," I said.

"Then you can go back to your room," she said, pointing to the door.

Not bad, I thought, as I escaped back to my class.

The second time was more ominous. We were taking a break in gym class. Bob and I were standing in a corner. The two of us had a complicated relationship. We weren't really friends but we did have something in common. Our bond was an adversarial one that had evolved from his anti-Semitism into the political arena. Bob was a staunch Republican while I espoused the views of the Democratic Party. He was also one of the smarter boys in the class and that created a special link.

When we were eleven, we took opposing positions in a classroom debate during the 1944 presidential campaign that pitted Franklin Roosevelt against Thomas Dewey. Bob was the major spokesman for Dewey.

"We need new leadership," he said. "FDR is old and sick. He is not fit to lead our country."

"Roosevelt is winning the war," I countered. "He has the right generals in Europe and the Pacific." I didn't add that he was beginning to defeat Hitler and that was of paramount importance.

"It's more than just about the war," Bob responded. "The New Deal has been expensive and wasteful. We need smaller government and less control of the economy. That's what Dewey stands for."

"You're wrong," I said. "The New Deal brought us out of the Depression and it is about the war. If we don't win it, we are doomed. Roosevelt can win this war." I paused and added the sentence that filled me with pride, "Let's not switch horses in the middle of the stream."

A debate to remember; at least, I remember it, I wonder if Bob remembered it that way? And did he remember the trouble we got in the next day?

Standing in the corner of the gym, we were conspirators carrying out a secretive mission. We were not in our usual adversarial mode. He looked around, reached furtively in his pocket, and pulled out a black and white picture of a naked man and woman in sharp focus and slipped it into my hand. The woman was standing, leaning forward against a table. The man stood behind her—what was he doing? I thought for only a moment. But it was clear what he was up to… I looked at Bob.

"Where'd you get it?" I asked. I was awestruck and fascinated. I'd never seen anything like that picture.

"My brother gave it to me," he whispered.

My eyes devoured the picture. It was like the roosters and hens in the chickenhouse but this was people. We were oblivious to danger approaching. Suddenly, I felt a tug from behind. It was the gym teacher. She had my shirt collar in one hand and Bob's in the other. The picture had disappeared into her pocket. She marched us out of the gym and I quickly guessed where we were going—to Gribbie's office.

We sat silently in the secretary's outer office while the two women conferred behind closed doors. Bob leaned toward me. "We're in for a whipping," he whispered. I nodded my head.

Gribbie came to the door and motioned me in alone. The gym teacher looked directly at me, shaking her head in serious disapproval. Gribbie's face was impassive. She sat down, ignoring the picture that was lying in the middle of her desk. I stood facing her. I waited for the strap to appear.

Wartime

RICHARD ROAD

RICHARD ROAD IS AN ACTUAL STREET in New Jersey's Monmouth County, a few miles outside of Farmingdale. It runs a half mile between West Farms Road and Peskin Road. I doubt most people had ever heard of any of these adjoining streets when I lived there, and for good reason. Their only purpose was to connect the little farms with their small world. Today, they are all well-cared-for macadam streets that wind through residential areas. All traces of the chicken farms have long ago disappeared.

Back in the World War II era, Richard Road still had a sand and gravel surface that was usually rutted and, most of the time, looked like an elongated washboard. A profusion of scrubby weeds grew along the road like unruly bystanders. At times, they were joined by wild flowers—violets, daisies, and goldenrod.

Large trucks delivering sacks of grain and mash for the area chicken farms or collecting heavy crates of eggs, avoided the side road except to visit the three farms served by the street. The egg trucks always drove slowly for fear of cracking the shells of their valuable cargo.

Twice each year a county road scraper, like a yellow-colored alien, would smooth out the road but the traffic would roughen it again within a week. Vehicles traveling down the road were always half hidden by the cloud of dust swirling around them. After a heavy rain, the dirt would turn into a muddy paste that splattered on our dust-covered car. Some years the school bus would travel the road; other years the school would have the buses avoid it. The few school kids living on the street would walk over to meet the bus up on the West Farms Road; their shoes usually covered with a fine film of road dust.

The mailman came down the road faithfully six days each week, connecting us with the outside world. "RD 1, Box 125" was painstakingly stenciled in black letters on the side of the mailbox which was painted white but dulled by the perpetual road dust. It regularly contained such treasures as the *Aufbau*, directed at the German Jewish immigrants, and the *Freehold Transcript*, both weekly newspapers that arrived on Thursday. There were also the regular weekly magazines—the two that were always of special interest for me were *Life Magazine* with its vivid pictures of our soldiers fighting the war and the adventure stories in *Boys Life*.

Letters from relatives were greeted with great excitement. As the war years came closer, envelopes leaving Germany had been opened and marked censored by some unknown civil servant. I wanted Dad to look for coded secret messages but he said there weren't any. Finally, the censored letters stopped coming and the only ones were from New York. We placed outgoing mail neatly in the box and raised the red flag. It would alert the carrier that an important envelope was waiting for him to take.

Occasionally the sparse traffic would come to a halt. It

and the active part of their farm was in such great condition, but, as my mother said, "…they were in remarkably good shape compared to the ramshackle buildings across the road from us."

The poultry industry was big business in central New Jersey during the mid-1940s and Abe thought he knew how to capitalize on it. All the farmers were raising hens for the eggs—eggs were what it was all about. The baby roosters were culled out at the hatcheries and no one wanted them. Abe figured he would buy a few thousand baby roosters for next to nothing, raise them over the summer, and sell them as fryers in the fall. And that's what he tried to do, but even though they really did cost next to nothing, he still had to borrow the money to buy them. Abe was going to use the old, beat-up coops across the road to house his multitude of baby moneymakers.

"If it's such an easy way to make money," I asked, "why don't we do that too?"

Dad and I were down in the basement. We were both cleaning eggs with our sandpaper brushes. It was the usual daily routine in the late afternoon—removing dirt and dried droppings from each egg and then weighing and packing them in cases.

"It's not as simple as Abe thinks," Dad answered. "You have to feed them all spring and summer without any income and then you have to hope that the selling price for the roosters in the fall is high enough to pay your feed costs and give you a profit. Abe had to borrow the money for the chicks and for the feed, and he has to make enough to pay the interest, too. I think he's gambling."

"Maybe his parents would help him," I said.

"That's possible," Dad answered, "but when I drive past their farm, they don't seem to be doing so well." He paused, placing the egg he had just weighed into one of the packing cases. "It's hard to say."

No one ever got to know Abe's parents, the old Garfinkle couple. I don't think we ever met them in all the years they were our neighbors. Old man Garfinkle seemed ancient. He never talked to anyone but always gave a polite wave when he drove by in his old brown pick-up truck. Their son David was a year younger than me and had cerebral palsy and wasn't very smart. My mother said he was retarded, that was the polite term then; but now we'd call him learning disabled.

Abe was a lot older than his brother and not so smart either, but in a different way. Abe was a ne'er-do-well—a good old-fashioned term that really fit him. He was tall and lanky with long, black curly hair and a constant arrogant smirk painted on his face. He hadn't done well in school but always managed to have a girl riding around with him in his pick-up truck. My mother said his father kept him in trucks.

The girls, there were a number of different ones; all wore shorts, tight sweaters, and lots of red lipstick. He always had a deal going—a sure-fire moneymaker.

Abe's male baby chicks arrived about the same time as our female ones did. We housed ours comfortably in a specially-designed long white building called the "brooder house." Each room in the building had a centrally outfitted electric thermostat-controlled stove with a large octagonal hood under which several hundred baby chicks lived, protected from the cold of early spring. Abe borrowed some coal stoves from his dad—we had done away with coal years before—and boarded up the broken windows and covered the leaky areas on the roof with extra tarpaper to protect his roosters. We watched the developments across the road with interest.

By late spring, our fuzzy yellow baby chicks had turned into white-feathered pullets ready to spend the summer on the range, a meadow filled with small grasses range area, we constructed a chicken wire fence around the entire front and side of the farm. It was hard work and took two whole days. Dad built a sturdy wire-covered gate for the driveway. I spent hours painting it.

Dad and I went out the next morning to inspect the result of our efforts. A few of Abe's roosters were right there to meet us.

"Look at what they're doing," I exclaimed. "They're pecking the paint off the wood."

Dad shook his head. "Those roosters are so hungry, they'll eat anything."

Richard Road was more a rutted gravel lane than an actual street. It was not really a through road; it was only used by the three families living on it, the few trucks that did business with us, and the mail carrier. Abe's scraggily young roosters, the ones that had escaped the ramshackle coops, were a new addition to the roadway as they wandered aimlessly, vainly searching for food and water.

When the foul smell of rotting carcasses began to saturate the air, Dad went down to the County Board of Health. Dad wasn't pleased with the interview. "They drove out with me and looked the scene over from the road," he told us at dinner. "They were horrified and upset. They said they'd talk to Abe, but, at the same time, they had no jurisdiction in the matter—no jurisdiction to inspect his place, no jurisdiction to get involved in any way, no jurisdiction to prosecute. They say there's no human health risk."

Mom was aghast. "There's got to be something we can do," she exclaimed.

"Well, if there is, I haven't figured it out," Dad said. "I even talked to Abe last week and he told me to mind my own business. I think we've done everything I know to protect us. I'm even having drugs against coccidiosis put in our chickens' feed."

The next Saturday evening, my parents went to visit some friends and took Frank along. They'd have taken me too but they wanted someone to watch the farm.

"Just keep an eye on things," Mom instructed me. "If, by any chance, Abe tries to come over, you stay clear of him. Go inside and lock the doors. You call us and we'll be back in twenty minutes. You're only thirteen years old, so just stay away from him and don't talk with him. He's a worthless no-good bum so let your father handle him—if he comes—which he probably won't."

I sat with my feet dangling off the front porch listening to the radio I'd set up in the dining room window. The foul smell of dying roosters saturated the evening breeze. It must be like a concentration camp over there, I mused, a concentration camp for roosters. An hour must have gone by when, suddenly, Abe was standing outside the gate that stretched across the driveway. His unkempt black curly hair and stubbly beard gave him a sinister look. The only addition that would have made him seem more menacing might have been a black rectangular moustache. He was carrying a .22 rifle under his arm. He looked quietly at me and gave me his malevolent grin. He slowly unlatched the gate and sauntered down the driveway toward me, never moving the gun.

I was more angry than frightened. "Where's your father?" Abe demanded.

"He's in the chicken coops working," I answered.

"Go get him," he ordered.

"I don't think so," I answered. "He doesn't have time for a worthless, no-good bum like you."

"Well, you tell that son-of-a-bitch he needs to talk to me," Abe was angry, "Nobody turns me in to the Board of Health without having to do some big-time explaining."

He turned and marched off down the road, the gun now over his shoulder, leaving the gate flung wide open.

Animals. She'll get this straightened out in no time."

Blanche Cook arrived the next evening in a big black sedan—no lights or siren, but with the mark of authority, nonetheless. Like Emily, Blanche was short and plump but unlike Emily, she wasn't at all grandmotherly. She marched over to the barn where my father was coming to meet her. Blanche wore a khaki shirt and tight khaki pants. She almost looked like a man with her straight short cut hair and long business-like stride. And she wore a shiny pistol in a black holster on a black leather belt around her big hips. She looked very official to me and I was thrilled to see the pistol. She meant business.

"Sal," she said, "I'm Blanche and I got to tell you, it stinks around here."

By now Mom had joined them from the house and she was standing there, her hands on her hips, beaming. This was Mom's kind of woman.

"Let's go over there across the street and see what's up, although I got a pretty good idea. I've never smelled anything this bad. I don't know how you put up with it."

"Don't you need a warrant or something?" Dad asked. I knew Dad was worried about breaking a law—that's why he'd never gone over there to look for himself. The vision of the threatening state trooper was still fresh in his mind.

It was the only time I saw her smile. "I got the warrant right here," she said patting her gun.

They came back forty minutes later. Blanche looked grim and angry. If she was a dragon, she'd be spewing fire. Mom and Dad looked overwhelmed, like they'd just been to hell and back.

Blanche was livid. "That damn, worthless, no-good bum," she exclaimed, echoing Mom's opinion of Abe. "He's got thousands of dead roosters piled up on each other and the few that are still alive are scavenging the dead ones. The temperature in those coops has got to be over on hundred degrees. I can't believe it. I'm getting a court order to have this mess cleaned up and removed. Then I'm going to serve him with a warrant. I guarantee you he's spending the night in jail."

She shook hands with my Dad. She slammed the door of the car shut, backed out of the driveway, and headed down the dirt road in a cloud of dust. I never saw her again. Abe was about to get a taste of Blanche's justice.

THE BEACH

MOM NEVER EXPLAINED why going to the beach in the summer was important; just that it was healthy for my brother and me. She had many dictums and that was one you could be sure she would never go back on because she thought it was good for her, too. We knew how much it meant to her every time she said swimming in the ocean was, "a touch of heaven." In fact, she loved it and we loved it, too. Going to the beach was also a welcome break from the summer heat on the farm. All the usual kid activities—outrunning the waves, building complex forts in the sand, water fights that sometimes ended with tears— were memorable to us.

The only thing we didn't like was the walk to and from the train station.

Dad usually stayed at home to work but, when he went with us, it was better because we took the car. Mom didn't know how to drive a car then, although she was an expert in advising Dad. When Dad was too busy to come or there weren't enough coupons left on our gasoline ration card, he would drive us to the train station a few miles away. Wartime rationing on many products was in full force. As a farmer, Dad was eligible for the top quota amount for gasoline—the black "A" gasoline sticker displayed on the rear window—but the top quota was still not enough for regular visits to the beach.

When we waited for the train, I could hear the whistle long before the black engine appeared. At first, it was only a dark speck with a billow of smoke rising above as it rounded the last turn, heading into the long straightaway.

"You can just see it as it comes around the curve below Mrs. Michel's house," I said, trying to impress Mom.

"How do you know that?" she asked.

"Dad told me the last time we came to town," I answered. "You can just barely see the station when you cross the tracks by her house."

The train hissed to a stop in front of the small dusty red brick station. Its façade had long ago been blackened by soot and coal dust from years of steam trains. The engine looked like a fire-eating monster and its wheels, darkened by grime with bits of burnished steel shining through, towered over us. My eyes were fixed on the engineer standing on his platform in front of the tender filled with coal. He wore a darkly-stained striped cap that reminded me of Dad's feed company hats except for the gray and white color. With his hands on the controls of this huge monster, he seemed superhuman.

The conductor stepped down the steep steps of the passenger car, the silver whistle planted firmly between his teeth. He nodded at us and watched Frank and me scrabble up the high metal steps. He took the beach umbrella from Mom and, once she'd gotten into the car, handed it up to her.

"Thank you," she said. I'd convinced her to stop adding "mister." It made sense to her, as a translation from German, but it didn't convert well.

Moments later, I heard the conductor shout, "All aboard." He made it sound like one word: allaboard— the "d" rising and sounding like a "t."

Doors slammed shut. The five cars clanked together and then pulled apart as the train began to move.

The summer heat was oppressive enough outside but it was worse in the car. I could feel the damp sweat under my shirt as the wheels clattered along on the tracks, their accelerating sound punctuated by the blare of the engine whistle.

Even though we loved going to the beach, we still could find things to argue about with Mom. "Can't we open a window?" Frank would shout over the clatter of the iron wheels, "It's roasting in here." It was a lost cause. I knew the answer.

"The draft is bad for you," Mom would say, shaking her head. Then, almost as an afterthought, she would add, "And all that dirty smoke is bad for your lungs and it's unsanitary."

"Aw," Frank would yell back. Unsanitary, I thought, was one of Mom's favorite words.

I sat across from Mom and Frank in a high-backed leather seat in the otherwise empty car. The umbrella was tucked neatly behind me and the beach bags sat next to me. I pressed my nose against the cool window glass watching the houses and barns pass by. An occasional cow looked up, laconically chewing sideways, its curiosity aroused by rattling wheels and smoke.

In the heat of the passenger car, I thought about all the people staying in the bungalow colony the Hamburgers ran a mile from the farm on the West Farms Road. They came from New York City, Newark, and Jersey City for the summer. The family would stay all week while the father would work in the city and come out for the weekend. There was no air conditioning in those days. Big fans were the best solution we had to the summer heat—that and a big bowl of ice cream.

"Those Hamburger bungalows must be pretty hot.

Do you think the summer people go to the beach like we do?" I asked Mom. "I never see them on the train."

"I suppose some of them do," she answered, "but I think a lot of them just enjoy being out in the country away from the hot city. Coming to our farm to buy eggs is a special treat for them."

I knew Mom was right. The little children always got excited when they saw the chickens on the range. The parents would marvel at the egg cleaning and packing process. Dad called them city slickers.

Gradually the ocean smell intruded into the musty odor from the engine. The stops at Sea Girt and then Spring Lake seemed endless but finally the conductor announced, "Belmar." That was us. I looked back at the engineer standing on his platform. He waved at me and I felt suddenly proud. He knows who I am, I thought.

The fun part of the trip was over. For the next twenty minutes we walked the endless mile from the train stop to the beach. A one mile walk doesn't seem so far today but it was a major trip in those days—distances are twice as far for little legs, especially in the summer heat. It was a chore to lug a beach umbrella, beach toys, extra clothes, and towels. No backpacks then, we all carried beach bags.

"I can't go any further," Frank would complain. "I want to sit down and rest." He'd plump himself down on a beach bag and look sad. Where were Dad and the car when we needed them?

The drill was always the same; Mom would hand me the umbrella and grab Frank's arm, gently pulling him along. After all, he was four years younger than me. It'll be worse on the return trip, I would think, when we're tired and have the ocean behind us.

"It's too hot to walk," Frank would say in a whiney voice. "I can't go any further."

"He's right, Mom. Why couldn't Dad drive us today?"

water and the vastness of the ocean made it much safer. To learn to swim was to risk polio; that was her quandary.

"It can't make any difference," I tried to argue. "The salt water in the pool comes from the ocean. It's all the same."

"No it's not," she answered. "People sometimes do their business in the water. In the ocean, it gets washed away. In the pool it stays and can get in your mouth and nose. That's how germs are spread."

There was never winning an argument with Mom even though, this time, she was exactly right.

None of us knew—I didn't learn it until years later in medical school—that only one of a hundred people infected with the virus got the crippling form of polio. For Mom it was straightforward. If you got infected by the polio virus, paralysis followed. As it turned out, most people suffered only a bout of diarrhea and that just for a few days. Most of us probably had contracted it but who knew? Even if Mom had known the odds, she'd have felt the same. One out of a hundred is still a lot.

Mom finally decided to let us go—but only for our swimming lessons. Frank and I were enthralled by the idea of going to the pool.

"We have to practice here, too," I said knowing that argument would go nowhere, "that means more time in the pool." I couldn't resist. Mom's declarations invited disagreement. I was getting to the frequent and troublesome, "argument for argument's sake," stage with Mom.

"You can practice in the ocean."

"Yea, but look how rough it is today. Even you can't swim in it."

"It'll be better next time we come down."

"But we don't know when we'll come down again; it could be two weeks…" My voice trailed off; this was the last word Mom would tolerate from me, I could tell.

The next problem was the tar. Noone under sixty remembers it today but it was the way it was to us—we had never seen a clean beach.

There was no disagreement with Mom about the tar. We all hated it. Flecks of the black sticky stuff were scattered all along the beach as if flattened black jelly beans had been sprinkled over the hot, finely-granulated sand. Sometimes the tar appeared as large star-shaped globs— black holes at the ocean's edge. It stuck tenaciously to our feet, our legs, and our hands, like black glue. It was really nasty on bathing suits. There was no way to avoid it—it was a modern-day plague.

The tar had a serious and sinister overtone. "It's washed in by the tides," Mom explained. "It comes from the American oil tankers that the Nazi U-boats sink."

"Can the U-boats come to the beach and attack us?"

"They're not interested in us," Mom answered, "they want to sink the freighters full of oil and the ships that carry food and fighting equipment to England on Lend Lease."

Looking out at the ocean, I could often see large ships sitting on the horizon line. I watched them, worrying that they were oil tankers about to explode. I could picture huge blobs of black oil floating to our beach and turning into tar.

Frank and I secretly worried about the U-boats. We imagined black bearded men fiercely dashing onto the beach shouting at us, *"Achtung, achtung,"* the sound of Nazis attacking.

"Look," I would yell to Frank, "I can see a conning tower over there."

"I can't see it," he'd answer.

I'd watch in awe, waiting for the submarine hull to surface. It never did and the imagined conning towers would disappear.

Still, there was always the sticky tar. For me, its black-ness symbolized the evil of our mortal enemy. The Nazis were the bad guys. That Dad had fought in the German Army against the Americans twenty-five years earlier was totally unrelated—those guys fighting together with Dad were German, these guys we were fighting today were Nazis. This war was personal and the good and bad guys were clearly defined.

"Try not to step in the tar," Mom would say, but that was almost impossible. I would try tip-toeing around and through them but unseen flecks of black always managed to stick to my feet. Playing in the sand made it all the worse. By the end of the day, speckles of tar covered my legs and hands.

On the way home, there was the necessary stop on the boardwalk. The city had dispensers of kerosene attached to the wooden railing. Scrubbing off the tar with kerosene, with its evil smelly overtones, was almost as bad as the walk back to the train.

I liked going to the beach, nevertheless. The negatives never outweighed the experience. The cool water and the warm sand made the heat of the summer tolerable. But the tar—would there ever be a time when the sand would be free of this sticky black plague?

"Someday the tar will be gone," Mom would say as we trekked back to the train station, "but first, the American Navy will have to stop the U-boats from sinking our oil tankers."

The U-boats were the epitome of evil. Little cigar-shaped vessels that could hide under water and, in the darkness, sneak up to a ship and torpedo it.

"Dad says we haven't figured out how to stop them."

"Roosevelt will find a way," Mom replied, as if trying to convince herself. For her, he was the big hero and savior. Losing to the Nazis was unthinkable.

"Why don't we send out some planes and bomb or shoot those U-boats?" I asked.

"Maybe they will," Mom said, "but the ocean is so big…"

Before leaving the beach, there was another ritual—changing into a dry pair of shorts. Wet pants caused kidney infections, just like sitting on the cold concrete steps at home—another of Mom's dictums. We had to abide by them, or else.

A sign on the boardwalk stated the city ordinance clearly: "No disrobing on the beach." That meant renting a locker, an extravagance Mom said we could not afford. She would cover each of us, Frank usually first, with her huge maroon and white patterned terrycloth bathrobe while we changed. When Dad was there, I'd use his matching gray and white bathrobe. They were part of the shopping spree in Germany that Dad sent Mom on to spend some of the money that would otherwise have been left behind and lost.

"Mom, you know this is illegal. See the signs? We could all get arrested."

"Just be quiet and get it done," she said, "and don't get any tar on the towel." We never got caught; I didn't know most beachgoers were doing the same thing.

On the boardwalk, still under Mom's watchful eye, we would carefully wash off the flecks of tar and then rub off the kerosene with brown soap and water—Mom always brought the brown soap—before beginning the trudge back to the train station.

Mom said, "Stop walking barefoot on the boardwalk."

"Look at all the other kids. They're not wearing shoes. Why do I have to?" I was starting to get whiney again, leaving the beach was always a disappointment.

"You'll get splinters. And put your socks on. It's bad for the shoes if you don't wear socks."

I would reluctantly follow her admonition. When she was distracted by Frank I would try walking barefoot but I often did get splinters. That meant going through the painful ritual of Mom picking them out of the soles of my feet with a sewing needle when we got home. It wasn't worth it even though it felt good trying to be like the other kids.

Dad would always be waiting for us when the train arrived back in Farmingdale, being punctual was one of his great virtues. Once home, we participated in another of Mom's rituals (always with a lot of complaining). We complained about everything. We would pump a bucket full of cold water to soak our bathing trunks.

"It's important to get the salt out," Mom always said. "Salt destroys the material." Never mind that we outgrew them faster than any salt could eat them away—Mom's opinions never wavered. After complaining as we rinsed our trunks, we had to wring them out and hang them on the clothesline.

"They need to be dry in case the weather is nice and we go again tomorrow," Mom would say, but we knew it was just another of her rituals.

If it was Friday, there was my immediate response, accompanied by false-holy expressions that were really smirks, "But tomorrow is the Sabbath and we never drive on Saturday."

She would just look sternly at me. "You need to put more energy into wringing out your shorts and not answering back all the time. They're still full of water and so are you."

In describing this period of time with its tar-sprinkled beaches, Brian John Murphy wrote the following in the October 2006 issue of the magazine, *America in WWII*:

> *"For seven months, from mid-January to early August 1942, German U-boats would take control of America's East Coast waters, sinking freighters and oil and gasoline tankers—anything and everything steaming off the coast. Ship by sinking ship, the Nazis achieved a victory over the United States comparable to and even more devastating than the one the Japanese had enjoyed at Pearl Harbor a few weeks earlier.*
>
> *"The U-boats had scored the most one-sided and damaging victory against the United States of any foreign naval power. Germany had sunk 233 ships off the East Coast and in the Gulf of Mexico and killed no fewer than 5,000 seamen and passengers. The operation caused major disruptions in war-material production and in the shipping of supplies to the war fronts. This was Germany's first strategic victory of the war that directly impacted on the American homeland. Fortunately, it was also Germany's last."*

STORIES

THE HEAVILY-CARVED BOOKCASE which filled an entire wall in our parlor was not one of Mom's extravagant purchases before the trip to America; it was firmly in place in the newly-purchased farmhouse when we bought it. The prior owner said it was too bulky and cumbersome to move, and so he left it.

Mom's extensive collection of books brought from Germany stood behind its glass doors. Volumes by Goethe, Schiller, Heine, and Lessing were her prize possessions. To her, they were the great German writers. They stood in sharp contrast to the evil and immorality of Hitler's Third Reich. The velvety maroon leather book covers, the gold lettering, and the rich design made them the centerpiece in the bookshelf.

Mom's collection of children's books sat on a lower shelf. These, although less prominently displayed, were used a great deal more. A large volume of *Fairy Tales* by Jacob and Wilhelm Grimm with a fear-inspiring color picture of the wolf masquerading as the grandmother and sneering at Little Red Riding Hood was central.

Mom would read them out loud to me at bedtime, like it or not. I didn't like some of them.

"Mom," I said one day, "these are not funny or happy."

She stopped reading and looked at me.

"These are mean stories," I continued. "I hate the story of the girl with no hands. How can a father cut off his daughter's hands just because the devil demanded it?"

I decided not to mention the wolf devouring Little Red Riding Hood and her grandmother since we'd been over that one several times before. Even though they were saved by the Woodsman, the wolf's teeth appeared in my dreams.

"The stories are of mean witches and evil fairies," I said. "Just look at Hansel and Gretel, Rapunzel, and Snow White. Bad things are always happening. The worst is the story of the goose girl. The maid was a bad person, but to drag that woman down the street in a barrel of nails until she was dead? I don't like that."

Mom sighed. A.A. Milne's Winnie-the-Pooh had no equivalent in German literature. I suspect, thinking back, that she had never heard of him. The German stories were all about moralizing. The English stories were just fun.

"You are right," she said. "The German stories are very fierce and there is always cruelty in them—even though they have happy endings. The Scandinavian writers like Hans Christian Andersen are gentler." She was thinking of "The Ugly Duckling," one of her favorites and one we'd read before.

She was right. I liked some of them better. "But, Mom," I said, "what about the little match girl who froze? That one always makes me cry."

She patted me on the head. "Yes, it has a sad ending but Andersen's stories are not about mean people. The little girl has that wonderful dream about going to be with her beloved grandmother."

There were some German books I did like, one of the best was Struwwelpeter, which had marvelous pictures, especially the cover picture of a shaggy-haired boy with long spidery finger nails. His unkempt hair was like a disheveled halo around his head. It came with the usual moral—this time it was that scruffy boys have no friends.

Even the stories I liked were thick with morality but some seemed funny, like the fidgety boy who accidentally pulls all the food off the dinner table, and gets in trouble, of course, and the nasty boy who terrorizes animals only to get bitten by a dog that then eats the boy's sausages.

Others had cruel endings. A boy who wouldn't stop sucking his thumb has it snipped off by a tailor; a girl playing with matches burns to death; and a boy who won't eat his soup wastes away and dies. These were powerful retributions designed to terrorize a young boy and to guarantee compliance.

Mom treated the living room as if it were a formal library. Many farmhouses had parlors like ours, although not with such classical treasures inside. Mother protected our good furniture from both fading by the sun and damage by the children.

Our living room's glass-paned door was always closed and, when allowed inside, Frank and I would always speak in whispers. It was a place to read and listen to classical music—a place where Mom celebrated her former cultural life.

All the books were in German, none in English, and the recordings were all symphonies and concertos composed by the European masters. Mom's rule, except when we had company, was take your shoes off—we don't want to damage the Persian rugs—and no feet on the sofa, please, even without shoes.

On the wall overlooking the room was Mom's cherished engraving by William Hogarth, "Moses Brought to Pharaoh's Daughter." The picture showed Moses' mother being paid as she gives her son away.

"Why would a mother sell her son?" I asked after she explained the meaning of the picture one day. The idea was horrifying to me.

"It was a hard time for the Jews," she said. Then, after a pause, she added, "It's always a hard time for the Jews."

She gave me a wistful smile. "Pharaoh had ordered that all Jewish boys be killed," she said. "Pharaoh wanted to get rid of us. It was just like now."

That was even more appalling than Moses losing his mother. "His mother gave him up so he could survive," she said.

It scared me to think of losing my mother and living with strangers.

Mom squeezed my hand as we looked at it together. "It's a famous engraving. It hangs in London's Foundling Hospital, a place for children who've lost their parents."

Years later, I realized this masterpiece had a much deeper meaning for her than just another biblical scene about the repeated persecution of the Jews. It captured the essence of the epochal event in her own childhood, both losing her mother and being taken to the Babenhausen Waisenhaus. She wasn't an orphan; she was unwanted.

A favorite recording of Mom's was a collection of Brahms' Hungarian Dances played by the violinist, Erica Morini. She had been a child prodigy in Germany and America and a good friend of Maria Hilger, my violin teacher. They had both studied with the famous Otakar Sevcik in Vienna and, like Maria and her sisters, immigrated to the United States in the 1920s. Morini was a child virtuoso who had continued her successful career in the United States—a theme that always commanded Mom's respect and admiration.

One of the books that had a place in the oak bookcase was about two undisciplined boys who carried out a series of outrageous pranks. Mom liked the rhythm and the rhyming verses of "Max and Moritz" but not their appalling adventures.

Much to her chagrin, it turned out to be one of my favorites. In the first series of pranks, the boys tied crusts of bread together with thread and put their creation in an old widow's chicken yard. The chickens gobbled up the crusts and became fatally ensnared. I would never have thought of such an ingenious plot with any of our chickens, but I loved it. In another act of mischief, the boys secretly filled their teacher's pipe with gunpowder that had explosive results when he lit it. The sheer audacity of this series of verses was amazing to me.

The whole adventure was an amusing boyish fantasy. Mom thought otherwise.

"Those are two really bad boys," she said. "Such deplorable behavior is inexcusable. Their mother did not spank them often enough. They deserved to be finally ground up into food for ducks." Mom's imaginary punishments rivaled Grimm's.

"Mom," I protested, "it's only a story. I would never do such a thing to our chickens."

"I should hope not," she puffed.

To make it worse, I discovered the Katzenjammer Kids in the comics. They were the reincarnation of Max and Moritz. They, like their German predecessors, were equally full of unruly pranks. Their names, Hans and Fritz, were hardly a disguise as they rebelled against all authority, especially that of Momma and "der" captain and "der" inspector (the surrogate father and a school official).

Mom didn't like the pranks of Max and Moritz or those of Hans and Fritz. And she didn't like Wilhelm Busch, the creator of Max and Moritz, either. Like Richard Wagner, he was anti-Semitic, according to Mom. Years later, I pointed out to her that one of her favorite pieces of classical music, Richard Strauss' "Till Eulenspiegel" with its haunting French horn preface, was about a prankster whose mischievous deeds were similar to those of the two pairs of boys. Mom just harrumphed.

She was always quick to criticize things German but her ambivalence toward German culture was complicated. She liked American traditions and way of life but the parlor was dedicated to the past. American books and toys, magazines, radios, and newspapers—the accoutrements of our new life—had no place there and were all elsewhere in the house.

As I grew older, I spent hours reading the books recommended by Nell Meyers, the librarian at the Freehold Public Library. Mom had shared her hopes and plans for my future with Mrs. Meyers who became a willing participant in mentoring my education. The bookshelves in my bedroom gradually filled with the great classics for boys. *The Count of Monte Cristo, The Man in the Iron Mask, The Three Musketeers,* and *The Last of the Mohicans* were just a few of my favorites.

In the summer, while Dad shopped in Freehold, I would sit in the library reading adventure novels I'd pulled off the shelves. I may have fought with Mom over her rigid beliefs and rituals, but her love of literature was fast becoming one of my passions.

Mrs. Meyers got me interested in reading detective stories. "I know your mother favors the classics," she said one day, "but I think you should read this book of stories about Sherlock Holmes. Have you heard of him?"

"I think there was a movie but I haven't seen it," I said.

"Well," she said. "Arthur Conan Doyle has written several books and many short stories about him. Your mother says you like science and you'll find Mr. Holmes to be very scientific. When you get ready to leave you can check it out." It was the beginning of my love affair with the famous detective.

As I think back, both my mother and Sherlock Holmes' ways of reasoning are interesting to compare. Both were strong-minded, dominating people but, at the same time, the forces driving each of them stood in sharp contrast. Mom was obsessed by a complex set of beliefs and rituals that led her to "truths." Holmes, on the other hand, had no beliefs before the fact—he was consumed by the scientific method in deducing the truth. Even attempting a comparison of my mother with the great detective shows the power of her personality.

No matter how unswerving her beliefs were, however, or how forcefully she presented them, the use of facts to solve problems logically had the greatest appeal to me. I came to realize that this was the basis for much of my conflict with Mom. She was all about right or wrong and good or evil. Once she made up her mind, she manipulated the facts to fit her hypothesis.

She had decided, for example, that Uncle Ben should have been more aggressive in trying to bring his mother, Oma, to America, and she would ignore any information to the contrary. In doing so, Mom was violating one of Sherlock Holmes' most important rules—"It is a capital mistake to theorize before one has data. Insensibly one begins to twist facts to suit theories, instead of theories to suit facts."

I had come to understand that underneath all his angst and periods of depression, Dad was a logical thinker and, in that regard, I was more like him than Mom. Even though Mom often treated him as Holmes did Dr. Watson, and I'd wished he could stand up to her, he was still my role model when it came to thinking through problems. So it was no surprise that math and the sciences were my favorite courses in high school even though I enjoyed English literature and music as well.

ADVENTURES—RADIO AND REAL

THE RCA VICTOR RADIO, a major link with the world outside, had a central place in the kitchen. Another radio sat on a chair in my bedroom. My favorite programs were never of interest to Mom. Whether I listened to "Little Orphan Annie" or "The Green Hornet" seemed to matter little. We did discuss the products that came with them, however. General Mills sponsored "The Lone Ranger" and the all-American boy, "Jack Armstrong." We agreed on Cheerios—oat cereals were healthy. Wheaties were out—I never understood why—but Tom Mix's Ralston was fine. It may have been because Purina made some of our chicken feed. Ralston became a household breakfast staple—hot in the winter and shredded in summer. I wanted Captain Midnight's Ovaltine but Mom declared that Droste's and Nestlé's cocoa in milk was healthier.

The westerns and the adventure series' featured on the radio shows stood in sharp contrast with the German stories Mom had brought with her. They all had the same moral—that good always triumphs over evil—but gruesome violence was not inherent in them. No one was killed or maimed. Guns were shot out of the villain's hands but no one was ever seriously hurt. The American radio stories glorified honorable behavior in the face of

evil. The German authors focused on bad deeds that needed punishment. The differences illustrate two ways of
looking at life. The bad guy in the old German tale is the
most important character.

In the American stories, the hero is the guardian of law
and order. It was part of the German culture to focus on
the villain performing his misdeeds which, as Mom might
have pointed out, was horribly illustrated by the Second
World War and the events that led up to it. I did enjoy
reading Max and Moritz but the radio stories were
the best.

"Return with us now to those thrilling days of yester-
year. From out of the past come the thundering hoof beats
of the great horse, Sil-ver! The Lone Ranger."

The rich, resonant voice of the annnouncer that
usually exploded from my elaborate cathedral-style
Philco radio was turned down to a barely-perceptible
whisper. The radio sat imposingly on a yellow cane-bot-
tomed chair next to my bed. My mother had brought the
chair from Germany but the radio was U. S. made, 1931
vintage, and mine to use at proper times. This was not one
of them. Tonight, the masked man would have to deal not
just with outlaws but also Mom's curfew.

The carved brown wood box with black knobs contained more than vacuum tubes, capacitors, and resistors.
It was filled with voices, hoof beats, footsteps on creaking
wooden floors, pelting rainstorms, and gun shots that
came from the speaker, hidden behind a yellow damask
cloth. That Philco turned my bedroom into colorful western towns and never-ending prairies night after night.

I pulled the tan wool blanket with its white linen
duvet cover up over my head and snuggled up to listen
secretly. The voice of Fred Foy, WXYZ's announcer, was
barely audible in my cold and dark bedroom. Only the
dimly flickering lights from the black cylindrical kerosene

stove standing in the middle of the floor and the working tubes from the radio cast a soft orange glow in the darkness. It was the best half-hour of the day.

Outside, the January cold hovered over a thick layer of snow covering the ground. Coming home from school, Mrs. Applegate had turned to tell me, "You'll have to walk home from the corner. Your road hasn't been plowed so I can't drive down it."

The Richard Road always seemed the last one to be cleared of snow. I was glad Mom had made me wear my rubber boots over my shoes. Not that I minded getting snow in my shoes but Mom would be upset with my cold wet feet. I knew the litany—cold, wet feet are the cause of sniffles, colds, and other dire ailments.

The window shades, black as the nighttime sky, were pulled to the sill to prevent any light from my room telling German planes where to drop their bombs—if their planes ever got this far. Both windows were open an inch to allow any fumes from the kerosene burner to escape. The oil-burning furnace in the basement was turned off every evening after dinner to save on the expense and conserve oil for the war effort.

My mother's rules for staying up late were, "Sleep before midnight is the most valuable and you have to get up early for school," and, "No radio after 7:30." These rules were inviolate. Bedtime was the same hour every school night and the only exceptions were Friday and Saturday—and then only until eight.

"But it's the Lone Ranger," I would complain. "Can't I stay up just a half-hour later? It's only three nights a week."

"You need the sleep," she would reply. The answer was always the same.

The Friday night compromise was the best I could wheedle out of her. Friday was good but not enough.

So every Monday and Wednesday night, as I lay in bed, one ear was up against the hushed radio speaker and the other was tuned to any creaks on the stairs. As the last strains of the "William Tell Overture" and visions of galloping horses faded softly into the darkness, I could feel my heart racing with excitement. I knew what was coming. Tonight was to be a replay of how the Lone Ranger finds his great white stallion and, with the help of Tonto, tracks down the notorious Butch Cavendish gang. I had heard this tale many times, but never often enough.

Suddenly, there was a squeak on the stairs. It was faint. At first, I thought it was the radio but the Lone Ranger was nowhere near a creaky floor. I held my breath. Is it the cold night air playing tricks? The staircase adjusting to the temperature? Then it came again, a little closer. It must be Mom tip-toeing as silently as she could up the wood staircase to check on me. She knew it was Wednesday night and that the Lone Ranger was a powerful temptation.

I clicked the radio off and rolled over in bed. There was an almost inaudible tap on the door as she came quietly in. I lay still, breathing deeply. She leaned over and kissed me lightly on my forehead. I could barely see her outline in the faint glow from the heater.

Please don't touch the radio, I thought to myself. The case was still warm from the heat of the vacuum tubes. It would be a dead give-away. Please, please. . . She didn't. I was safe.

Finally the subdued murmur of her voice talking with Dad in the kitchen just below me floated up the stairs. I clicked the radio back on again. The episode was at its climax with guns shot out of the hands of the bad guys and, finally, the ever-thrilling question as the great white stallion rode away, "Who was that masked man?" and the authoritative answer from one of the onlookers, "That's..." a pause, "...the Lone Ranger." And then the final note from the announcer as the theme music swelled and faded, "The Lone Ranger rides again."

The early 1940s were tumultuous times for all of us. The world was at war with Nazi Germany and the Japanese empire. Even though we believed we would win, the future of civilization seemed uncertain. It was important to have heroes. And in the stillness of the winter evening, the Lone Ranger fought the bad guys with daring, courage, and determination. And he always won.

The distinctive voice of Fred Foy announced the program and set the mood for the half hour show. Beginning in a steady, uniform tone that graduated in strength:

"He led the fight for law and order in the early western United States. Nowhere in the pages of history can one find a greater..." and when he reached the words, "...champion of justice," his voice rang with supreme conviction. Thrilling.

For a young boy, the message was clear—good would triumph over evil. For a moment, order had been restored. The knowledge made sleep come easily.

The Lone Ranger wasn't the only hero, just the most serious and convincing in my young world. War filled my imagination.

The Focke Wulf fighter was right behind me—right on my tail. I turned the steering wheel of my plane to the left just like Dad when he drove the Chevy. The German fighter turned with me. Suddenly, the steering was frozen. The wheel was stuck. It would only be seconds before the bullets would hit. When they came they sounded like three loud knocks on a door—then three more.

Mom was leaning over me, kissing my forehead. The brightness of the morning sun streamed through the bedroom window.

"Time to get up," she said. "The bus will be here soon.

Your favorite cereal is ready and so is a piece of marble cake."

I jumped out of bed and headed for the bathroom. I'd been sick all week with coughing and wheezing. It was exciting to be going back to school. Today there would be no mustard plasters on my chest and no lying with a towel tented over my head breathing steamy vapors rising from bowls of hot chamomile-laced water. My chest still burns with the memory of hot mustard paste leaking over the edge of the white cloth.

"Mom," I would yell. She was just below my bedroom in the kitchen. "The mustard is leaking all over. It's burning a hole in my skin."

Up the stairs she would tromp and check the plaster. To my relief she would usually say, "I think you've had enough."

She would carefully roll the soggy package up and take it with her.

"You know, my cough is no better after I've had it on my chest."

"It opens up the bronchial tree and helps get rid of the bronchitis." The words trailed behind her as she went back downstairs. She must have read that somewhere.

Getting dressed, I stopped to admire the picture of a huge B-17 bomber—the flying fortress—under the glass top of my nightstand. Planes were the special weapons of this war. The Navy ships, destroyers and PT boats were exciting too, but nothing rivaled flying. When I was sick I waited patiently each afternoon for the stirring words from the radio.

"CX4 to Control.....CX4 to Control......This is Hop Harrigan....coming in." A fighter plane roared in the background. The control tower answered, "Control Tower to CX4: Wind southeast, ceiling 1200, all clear." Hop Harrigan, the ace of the airways with his mechanic sidekick, Tank Tinker, were off on another adventure, flying with the Army Air Corps.

"What was it like being a soldier?" I asked Dad over breakfast. I knew that he'd fought in the German infantry in the First World War. He cut two big slabs of cheese and a chunk of wurst, putting them on his black bread. I was eating my hot Ralston cereal—Tom Mix's favorite breakfast—while Mom was serving Dad a hot cup of coffee.

"Nothing to tell. Being a soldier and fighting a war isn't fun." That's what he always said when I asked him about being in the army.

Dad put on his coat and went out to start the chores. Mom sat down at the kitchen table with her cup of coffee. "You know Dad doesn't like talking about the war." I nodded, I certainly knew that. Mom continued, "Just before that war ended, Dad leaned his gun against a tree and left, walking for days to get home. You must remember the story about your Uncle Ernst during the First World War?" It had become a family legend—Mom had told it often enough. Like Dad and Uncle Friedl, Ernst had fought for Germany in World War I long before I was born. I knew she'd tell it again if I kept quiet and waited.

"Ernst and his comrades were running across the battlefield. They were surrounded by rifle fire. Flares lit up the gray countryside. Ernst jumped into a trench he thought was empty, only to find an English soldier who was vainly trying to stem the bleeding from a shoulder wound. He was hunched over in the mud, his helmet and gun lay beside him. Ernst's rifle was drawn and he pointed it directly at his enemy—bayonet fixed. The Englishman sensed his end was near. He began to recite the Shema, the holiest of all the prayers in Judaism. 'Hear O Israel: the Lord our God, the Lord is one.'

"It was only a fleeting moment as Ernst had watched this frightened man, but he knew in his heart that he, too, would recite the same prayer in the final seconds of his own life. The eyes of the two men locked and a faint recognition passed between them. Slowly, Ernst raised his hand in a silent salute—and was gone." Mom always got teary at the end of the story.

My view of the war—the infantry war—was through the eyes of Ernie Pyle, the Pulitzer Prize winning war correspondent. When his new book, "Brave Men," was published in 1944, the librarian at the public library had Mom borrow it. After reading it, she bought a copy for us.

"You need to read it if you want to know what the life of a soldier is all about," she told me. "He has lived with them and knows all the horrors and terrors of war."

The book sat on my nightstand for months. I think I read it twice. War lost all its glamour. It became a world filled with freezing rain, men trudging through muddy fields, and shattered bodies. At night the soldiers hid in their foxholes, waiting for an enemy soldier to stumble by. They were all brave men but always cold and wet. War had lost its glamour.

I heard the milk bubble on the stove. "Mom, you let it boil over again," I yelled. "I'm not going to eat the skin."

"I'm sorry it overheated," she said, "but I can't throw the skin away. It's the healthiest part of the milk. I'll put an extra cookie in your lunch."

I didn't argue. I'd done that too many times before—not just about the skin but about the need to warm milk up. Mom said cold milk was not good for me; it would be an attack on my kidneys.

As I waited at the end of our driveway for the bus, I remembered a story Mom had told me about one experience Dad had in the war. It fit right in with Ernie Pyle's book except Dad was a German.

He had been fighting the Russians in the Ukraine and had gotten lost from his comrades. It was late afternoon and he was cold, dirty, and exhausted—he hadn't seen the sun in days because they'd been moving at night. As he plodded through the dark forest, he pictured his mother and father.

"I wonder if I'll ever see them again?" he thought. His boot struck the edge of a gnarled tree root that arched up out of the ground. Suddenly he lay in the damp rotting leaves of the forest floor, his knapsack still firmly on his back. For a moment, he imagined he was home lying in his bed but the musty dampness seeping through his jacket was enough to convince him to get up.

He wiped his hands on his pants. They were covered with bits of mud and fragments of decaying leaves. A few flecks of blood seeped from the scratches on his palms. This time he smeared his hands across his jacket.

"I'm glad I really didn't hurt myself," he heard himself say out loud. He walked slowly toward a clearing, leaning on his rifle, now turned walking stick.

A field that a few months earlier grew cabbages and potatoes was now pock-marked after the late fall harvest as if bombarded by hundreds of stick hand grenades. Dad didn't see the house until he was almost upon it. The graying wood timbers seemed a part of the desolate forest. Besides, Sally was intently searching the field for a last surviving cabbage plant or a few forgotten potatoes.

A tiny elderly woman, her shoulders stooped from years of toil, appeared from the side of the house and, not looking around, entered the house. "I need to be careful," he thought, stepping back behind a clump of trees. "I don't want to die in this forsaken forest."

It was then that he noticed a shed near the house. The woman had been coming from that direction. "Maybe I can get in after dark and find some dry hay to sleep on. There might even be a few potatoes to eat." He worried there might be a dog but, so far, he hadn't heard a bark.

"If there had been a dog," he mumbled, trying to reassure himself, "he's probably been eaten long ago."

The overcast day had promised rain and now it began as a light drizzle. Sally wasn't sure he wanted to wait a few more hours. He watched as a wisp of smoke began curling up from the chimney.

She's busy building a fire, Sally thought. Now is the time to sneak over to the shed. He walked silently, crouching forward. As he crept along next to the house, he kept his head below the only window. Suddenly, the faint gleam of a tarnished brass object nailed to the door frame caught his attention.

He stopped. He knew what it was without looking closely. He had seen it hundreds of times in Germany and now here was one far away and deep in the Ukrainian countryside. It was a mezuzah—a small brass case containing the Shema written on a bit of parchment.

He decided to forget the shed and headed straight for the door. It opened part way a moment after he knocked. The thin, wizened woman stood, her body hunched, watching the bedraggled soldier standing before her. "He's just a boy," she thought. "He could be my grandson." She recognized the foreign uniform but felt no fear.

Sally leaned his gun against the wall. The old woman stared at him, her lids hanging low over her eyes. A plain brown scarf, tied tightly, covered her head, as if to ward off the damp cold of the sodden fall day.

"Shalom Aleichem," he said, trying to smile.

"Shalom Aleichem," she answered. A thin smile spread across her furrowed face. The Russian soldiers, when they came to her house, just shouted commands for food at her. This boy used the words of the Sabbath song, "Peace be upon you."

She opened the door wide. Sally could see a fire in the huge stone fireplace. The warm dry air coming from the large open room felt comforting against his face. He followed her in. There seemed to be no one else in the house.

She pulled a wooden tub from a hidden corner and poured hot water into it from a kettle that hung over the fire. She added some cold water and waited. He dropped his clothes on the floor and climbed in. It was the first time he had felt warm in days. He didn't know how long he dozed but the smell of steaming cabbage crowded out his reverie of home.

Wrapped in an old dressing gown he ate a warming meal of cabbage and potatoes garnished with a sliver of meat. Sally couldn't remember a better dinner. Afterwards she led him to a straw-filled bed. He was already asleep when she put a blanket over him.

It was still dark when he awoke but a glimmer of morning shone through the window near him, the embers of the fire still warming the room. His uniform, washed and dry, hung from the far end of the fireplace. He dressed quickly and put on his backpack. The old grandmother slept on the floor by the hearth. Sally paused for a moment, then stepped outside and closed the door. He picked up his rifle, still leaning against the wall of the house, and left. That afternoon he found a battalion of German soldiers and joined them.

My memory of Dad's World War I story was interrupted by the arrival of my school bus. It had stopped at the foot of the driveway. Mrs. Applegate smiled as I climbed up the steep steps. She must have finally decided I was okay. I sat down in the front seat as the door shut, but my mind was still on Dad in Germany. I was glad the old woman in the forest took care of him—maybe even saved his life. But the story was confusing to me. Fighting a war was supposed to be glorious and it was about good guys and bad guys. Dad was a good guy, I thought, but at that time he was fighting on the side of the Germans who were the good guys then (or, were they?) and the enemy this time. So why weren't they the enemy then too? The old woman didn't seem to care who was who. When I'd asked Mom about it, she said that some things were more important.

"Someone recently said—I think it was in the *Aufbau*—that, despite what Hitler claimed, there were no bad Jews in Germany," Mom answered. "All Jews had at least one Christian friend who would testify to their goodness and that they were the exception to the Nazi dictum. When you get to know a person well, you will always find some good in them. But humans are predators—beasts of prey. The world is a cruel place, especially for us Jews and we have to stick together, no matter what country we're in."

Dissonance and Harmony

BECOMING A MAN

THE SYNAGOGUE IN FARMINGDALE didn't have a Hebrew Sunday school so the choices were either Freehold or Lakewood, the two nearby larger towns. Mom picked Lakewood's much more orthodox synagogue where I learned all the stories of the Old Testament—Jacob's deception of his father, the brothers selling Joseph into slavery, Lot's wife turned to salt. The war was still on full force and the lines from the Book of Isaiah, "they will beat their swords into plowshares and their spears into pruning hooks, and they shall not know war anymore," came as a revelation. Someone needs to tell the Germans and the Japanese, I thought.

I learned how to read and chant Hebrew. Traditionally, it was never taught as a foreign language with words that had meanings—just how to read it—which made it much less fun. The first prayer I had learned was long before the bar mitzvah preparation and that was the Shema—"Hear, O Israel. The Lord is our God, the Lord is one." Standing next to my father in synagogue, I had recited it hundreds of times.

Until the upcoming bar mitzvah, it was just a chant but now it took on more meaning. Buried in the prayer was the focus on the commandments that included: "And you shall bind them as a sign upon your arm, and they shall be as frontlets between your eyes. And you shall write them on the doorposts of your house and on your gates." When we were taught about posting the Shema on the doorpost, I remembered the story about my Dad in Russia and how seeing a brass mezuzah that contained the prayer on the Russian woman's door made it safe for Dad to knock and get help.

To me, posting prayers on the door frames was the easy part. Every door in the house had a mezuzah. Binding the commandments on my arm and forehead proved to be a more difficult matter. Putting on the tefill-in—the phylacteries—every morning in my bedroom was a complicated ritual. The tefillin were a pair of black leather boxes containing scrolls of parchment inscribed with biblical verses. Each box had long leather straps to bind one to my arm and the other on my head. And prayers had to be recited. The tefillin made me look like a foreign creature, not like the all-American boy I aspired to be, and I avoided looking in my bedroom mirror. I knew it would not be long before I broke one of the commandments, like lying to my mother when she'd ask me about completing the morning chore.

Now there was more Hebrew to learn. My major near-term goal was getting ready for my bar mitzvah. I worked hard preparing for it—memorizing all the prayers and readings I would have to recite in front of the whole congregation on Saturday morning.

"I'm so proud of you," my mother said. "You are really taking this seriously."

"It's important," I replied. I knew, to Dad, his oldest son becoming a man was especially important. I was also focused on the good time to come. It would be a big affair, a great family party, and that meant lots of presents. Presents, they were important, too.

"I guess we're going to drive on Saturday after all," I told my mother, knowing we couldn't walk the ten miles to Lakewood. For a moment, it seemed like a victory in our war of words over the orthodox rituals.

"Not at all," she answered. "We'll stay overnight at the kosher hotel, the Lieberman, in Lakewood and have a nice dinner there for everyone, with matzo ball soup, stewed chicken with all the trimmings, everything you want. It's all arranged."

"That's gonna' be real expensive," I exclaimed, astonished and a bit deflated.

I was reminded of Dad taking George Matthews out for dinner at the American Hotel after the citizenship rite at the courthouse. This would be even more extravagant but, at least, it was kosher.

"It's a momentous event, son" she replied. "You are going to become a man."

"Well, I guess," I said, still thinking of all the Hebrew left to learn, "but I'll really be a man when I finally get my driver's license." Mom just grimaced.

Dad had bought the red Ford pickup truck from George Mathews the year before. Dulled and tarnished from being in the heat, rain, and cold, it usually stood in the shade of the chickenhouse feed room. The truck sagged under the weight of the hundred-pound sacks of grain that it usually carried around the farm.

I was still three years away from getting a driver's license but Dad decided to teach me how to drive it. "The boy can't do much damage," he told Mom, "since he can't go very far." Driving off the farm onto Richard Road was an inviolate no-no especially since the truck didn't have a license. Jewish tradition says a boy becomes a man when he attains his bar mitzvah but as far as I was concerned, Dad letting me drive the truck was the first step in determining my manhood.

The baby chicks had turned into pullets and they would spend the summer on the fenced-in range until they began laying eggs. Late every afternoon, Frank and I would load up the truck with several one hundred pound bags of grain. The chickens were always ready. A thousand of them, a mass of white feathers, lined up along the wire fence eagerly waiting our truck when we drove through the gate. With the horde of chickens following us, my brother would slowly let out the feed as I drove the truck around the range spelling a different word each day—words like ball, peace, and mom.

I imagined the astonishment of a pilot flying overhead seeing the brilliantly white chicken-encrusted words painted on our field. My dad watched silently, shaking his head, trying not to smile. My mom dismissed it all with a droll, "my play babies are at work again." Bar mitzvah or no bar mitzvah, she knew her oldest son was long from being a man.

SPORTS

MY NON-ATHLETICISM had always been my personal humiliation. I wanted to be as adept at sports as my grade-school classmates but I had little success. Being good in the class room was easy but, on the playground or in gym class, success was impossible to achieve. I was always the last boy to be picked for a baseball team. I was poor at bat—though I practiced incessantly with Frank at home—and at throwing the ball in from the outfield. Basketball was a disaster. My dribbling skills were awful and it seemed like luck when I hit a basket.

I was good at dodge ball. I could move fast and avoid being hit. And I was good at running away on the playground when I was being chased by the school bullies. My talents at singing and playing the violin were no help. The girls seemed to approve but that did not help my status with the boys.

Ted Williams, Joe DiMaggio, Hank Greenberg—these were my boyhood heroes. I dreamed of hitting and fielding as they did but my clumsy efforts on the playground never fulfilled my daydreams. I knew I could run and that took no skill. Maybe when I got to high school, I thought, where they have track and cross country teams, maybe running could be my sport.

a lot—long distance training had not yet progressed to running five to ten miles daily—but I really liked my coach. And it would get me out of having to deal with Coach Goodwin in the fall. One positive cancelling out a negative, what more could I want?

The hard work paid off. By my senior year I had become the lead runner on the cross country team and the track team's best half miler. It was early spring when Coach Al Bennett asked me to be a member of the relay team he was entering in the Penn Relays. The prospect of running in Franklin Field was exciting.

The morning of the race finally came. As I parked my car, I could see Coach Bennett sitting patiently in his car outside the school, smoking his pipe, a wispy column of smoke rising from the open window. The early morning fog enhanced the calm silence of the otherwise empty school parking lot. Over the next few minutes, three other cars quietly rolled in and parked near his car. There was none of the weekday squealing of tires as students spun their cars into parking spots. Al must have smiled as the three boys pulled up, knowing they had made their share of noise on other days, but not this morning. He was glad to see they were in a subdued and sober mood.

"Good morning, Coach," I said as I got into the back seat. Carl, Tommy, and Willie were walking toward us. Coach Bennett nodded at me as he blew a small stream of smoke out the window. When we were settled into our seats, he turned the key in the ignition and put out his pipe. The trip to Philadelphia took less than an hour but the world we entered was new.

The four of us—three seniors and one junior—stood awestruck on the edge of the cinder track in Franklin Field, the stadium at the University of Pennsylvania. We looked up and around at the giant concrete structure. It was nothing like the bleachers that sat alongside the high school tracks where we had run our local races. The recognition that we were running in the big time—the Penn Relays—came crashing in to us, like a meteor from outer space. Our coach wandered off, cool as always.

I looked admiringly at my schoolmates. Their trim, fit bodies, like mine, were covered over by their light gray sweat suits emblazoned with the name of the high school. We looked like a team. I looked over at Coach Bennett.

The stadium was almost empty and he was sitting a few rows up from the finish line. His gray crew cut hair blended with the smoke from his pipe.

I was the only half-miler of the group but Coach Bennett had picked me as the fourth member of this elite quarter-mile relay team. For the last two weeks we'd practiced baton-passing every day. Dropping it during the hand-off was the ultimate sin. We started out doing blind passing, the receiver running the next leg would be facing down the track—looking away and waiting for his teammate to place it in his hand. As soon as he felt it there he would take off. The trouble was one or another of us kept dropping the baton.

Three days before the race Coach Bennett announced, "This will never work. No more blind passing—the guy receiving the baton is going to turn and watch for the hand-off. We'll lose a second or so while the runner turns back and takes off but it'll be safer."

The coach was right. The hand-offs went almost flawlessly. I dropped it the first time but not after that.

We sat in intense silence on the front tier as things got started. The trance of watching the early morning races that preceded ours was finally broken when Coach shouted from above us that it was time to warm up. The field was full of runners warming up and races were being run constantly. We stepped onto the track and did two easy laps around the outer edge, occasionally breaking into brief sprints, and then began the ritual of our stretching exercises. No one talked about it, but each of us thought about the afternoons of baton practice earlier in the week. Drop the baton and the race was over. Coach's last words to us as we entered the stadium were, "Just make sure the guy you're passing off to has a firm grip before you let go. If you do that right, you've got a good chance of winning the championship."

It seemed forever but, finally, the call for our race came. We slowly peeled off our sweat suits and passed them up to the coach who was now standing in the first row, just above us, at the starting line. We were now in our blue shorts and yellow jerseys, our faces and arms covered with a fine sheen of sweat that shimmered in the bright morning sun. We stood expectantly on the grassy infield along the inside of the track. Nobody talked—each of us was engrossed in private thoughts. I was tense but ready to run.

It seemed only a matter of seconds before Carl, our lead-off runner, lined up with five other runners. Carl took his position in the third lane on the track, the baton firmly clutched in his right hand. There were the usual instructions about not jumping the gun. Each runner leaned forward, not moving a muscle, until the gun went off. It seemed to take forever.

There was a scramble of six runners around the first turn. In the backstretch, Carl's short, powerful body hurtled to the front of the pack. His muscular legs churned like powerful pistons as he maintained the lead. Approaching the finish line he was five yards out in front. Willie was waiting for him, his right arm outstretched.

"Please don't drop it, Willie," I thought. The handoff was crisp and smooth and Willie was off. I watched him hold the lead until he sprinted down the backstretch, a pure power runner adding another yard to the lead.

It was time for me to move onto the track. The other runners waiting to run the third leg of the race gave me the inside lane as Willie streaked into the last fifty yards.

I reached my right hand in his direction waiting to grab the baton. "Come on, Willie," I thought but almost screamed it, and then whispered to myself, "Don't drop it when he gives it to you and especially when you switch it to your left hand."

His glistening body leaned forward as he stretched the baton in front of him. I grasped it firmly and was off.

I was in first place in Franklin field and my legs were driving as fast as I could move them. Around the first turn, the back straight-away, and through the second turn, I was still in first place. Coming out of the backstretch I could hear someone closing in on me. I knew not to look—coach had strongly chastised me the year before when I lost a race just at the finish line. I kept my head down and charged forward. He passed me in the home-stretch. I sprinted as hard as I could—my legs beginning to feel heavy—but he maintained the lead. Passing the baton suddenly became my single focus. Tommy stretched his right arm back to meet the baton and then he was away.

I fell on the grass on the edge of the track, buried my face in the grass, and sobbed. I had committed the ultimate sin—I had lost the lead and let my teammates down. Carl and Willie stood quietly nearby. Suddenly, I heard them yelling. I looked up and watched Tommy move back into first place. The crying was over. My tears of desperation were now tears of joy. "Oh, please, Tommy, please take it all the way." I was on my feet joining in the cheering. Tommy just kept widening the lead and hit the finish line with ten yards to spare. We'd won.

I laughed and cried all at the same time as we hugged each other and all of a sudden Coach was there. Al

Bennett didn't smile very often but now his face was one huge grin—not a word from him, his grin said it. His stopwatch now hung loosely around his neck. I knew he would have all the times for us later.

On the way home he told us, "You guys were great. Every one of you ran the best quarter mile of your life." Then, looking at me he added, "The team I was worried about ran their fastest man in the third leg against Lud and their slowest last against Tommy. They wanted to give their slow guy an insurmountable lead. Their strategy didn't work." He didn't add how well I did against that speedy guy; he didn't need to, the times showed it clearly.

Riding back, it seemed like a spectacular dream but the round gold medal with its blue and red ribbon was real. Emblazoned in gold was Benjamin Franklin, seated in an armchair, shaking hands with four lithe athletes. I closed my eyes and imagined they were us.

Once the excitement of the win at the Franklin Field was over, we were back practicing for our dual meets with other area high schools. Coach Bennett's emphasis on speed work paid off as I began winning my races.

"Your times are getting down there," he said late in practice one day. "I'm going to enter you in the 880 state finals."

A few days later, as I came out of the locker room, Coach Goodwin stood just outside the open door of his office. "I'm going to be in my office for a while," he said, looking at me. "When you get done with practice, I'd like to talk with you." The last time Coach Goodwin had ever talked with me was in my freshman year and that was more of a warning than a conversation. I knew what to expect and I didn't expect much more.

"Sure," I answered as I went into the gym to begin

my stretching exercises. Today Coach Bennett would have me doing speed work, getting ready for the next two dual meets before the finals.

My senior year was turning into a success. Not only had I been a member of the relay team that took a first place at the Penn Relays, but I'd won in the 880 yard runs in most of our meets. In the fall, I'd been the lead runner on the cross country team and had placed in the top ten in the state finals, but my breakthrough was a year earlier, when I was a junior.

The first cross country meet of that season was against Asbury Park High School. Our star runner, Sal, was out with a hamstring injury. Coach Bennett thought Asbury Park, with three premier runners, would humiliate us. Just before the race Coach DeMott took me aside.

"You've looked good in practice this year," he said. "Try to stay up with the leaders. You've got a chance."

The course was around a large golf course and on a path through some woods. I ran hard and did what the coach told me—stayed with the pack of three front runners. Coach DeMott had stationed himself on the last turn with a half mile left to go. He didn't say a word, just nodded at me. I was in second place, a few steps behind the leader. When Coach Bennett, standing at the finish line, saw me in second place, he screamed, "Take him." I tried but my legs were tired and heavy. I settled for second place. "Pretty good," he said and patted me on the back. I knew he was pleased. My strong finish had avoided a disastrous defeat for our team.

Now it was time to prepare for practice. As I began my hamstring stretches, I wondered why Coach Goodwin wanted to see me when I finished. He was the director of physical education and he came across to us as a tough, intimidating man, much like a battle-hardened marine drill sergeant. I didn't think he had much interest in me.

I remember him telling me I was a disaster as an athlete when I was a freshman and wanted to try for the track team. It was still clear in my memory. I thought it had been an attempt to intimidate me, perhaps, or he was just fed up with guys trying to get out of his phys ed class.

He hasn't paid much attention to me since that conversation, I thought. I'm almost finished with high school. It's curious he wants to talk with me now.

I finished my interval running under Al Bennett's watchful eye and went to the athletic office before taking my shower. I was getting anxious to hear what Coach Goodwin had to say. "Come on in and have a seat, son," he said, pointing to the only other chair, beside his in the room. My legs were sore from all the interval sprints and the sweat was pouring off me. I eased myself into the chair. Coach Goodwin didn't seem to notice.

"I watched you work today," he said. "You've come a long way in the last four years. You can really move on the track. Coach Bennett is real proud of you."

"Thanks," I said and waited. He leaned back. The dour look on his face was locked in place, even in praise.

"I know Bennett has entered you in the 880 state finals next month and he thinks you have a shot at placing among the top finishers. He told me he couldn't get there till late in the morning. I'd be real pleased to drive you up so you can get there early."

I smiled and nodded. I had really wanted Mom and Dad to drive there with me.

"It's on Saturday," Mom had said. "You know we can't drive on the Sabbath."

"But it'll be the biggest race of my life. You've never seen me in a race. Can't you make an exception just once?" I implored.

"It's bad enough that you have to drive," she said, patting my shoulder. "I'm sorry."

Watching Coach Goodwin look back down at the manual he was marking up, I suddenly realized he had been watching my progress these last four years, just as he said he would, and he was proud of me. Of course, he never would have admitted that. Still, not bad, I thought.

CONFLICTS

MY EARLY HIGH SCHOOL YEARS were spent in constant battle with Mom. Her powerful return to religion after the family's escape from Nazi Germany was a large part of it. Her pact with God wasn't my promise; but there was more. Mom had a judgmental style that served all situations; all things were right or wrong and people were all either good or bad. This ran directly counter to my thinking and was impossible for me to take.

She thrived on rituals that may have come from her years of growing up in an orphanage. And she had a whole host of beliefs that had no scientific basis. She did acknowledge that the earth was round and revolved around the sun but it all went downhill from there.

Mom and I would have gotten along much better if God had not decreed Saturday the day of rest or had made baseball, driving, and writing exceptions to His law. Still, she decided, a bargain was a bargain. We had all gotten safely out of Germany. And we did it with divine help as far as she was concerned.

"The Bible says the Jews are God's special people and, if we worship him, he will take care of us," she told me.

"Then why have so many bad things happened to us?" I asked.

"It's because we have not always obeyed his laws and commandments," she replied.

The clashes often occurred after school but following my afternoon snack. She never used food as a weapon. There was always one of Mom's homemade cakes or pies waiting for me. Streusel kuchen (crumb cake) was my favorite and Mom managed to bake it often. Her fruit pies were pretty good, too. What often wasn't so good was the warm milk that came with the cake.

"Mom, why can't I drink the milk cold?" I would ask.

"It's not healthy," she would reply. "It's bad for your kidneys."

"I get to drink it cold at school and I like it better."

"Well, cold milk is not good for you and you won't get it in our house."

"OK," I would answer. "Warm is all right but I hate it when it's boiled."

I knew she never meant to boil it but when she was busy, she would forget and let it overheat. And that happened all too often, so the litany repeated itself all too often.

Boiled milk comes with a slimy membrane on top like a piece of wet wrinkled skin. "Let's get rid of this thing," I'd say, holding it up, dripping, on the end of my spoon. "It tastes terrible."

"No," she'd answer, "it's the best part of the milk. You'll have to eat it."

"And, while I'm thinking of it, don't sit on the cement steps of the back porch. Cold causes kidney infections. How many times do I have to tell you that?"

If it wasn't about the kidneys, it was about the lungs, or the value of before midnight sleep. We were having the same argument for the umpteenth time.

"I asked my biology teacher about it and he says you're wrong," I said.

"Well," she answered, "He's not a doctor. Besides, cold is not good for the kidneys."

"I asked Dr. Lewis and he never heard of it either."

"I think you made that up," she said. I smiled—she was right that time.

Money was contaminated by germs, according to Mom; the result of many people handling it. She insisted that we all wash our hands after touching coins. That actually made sense to me until a high school biology lab experiment.

Each pair of students had a Petri dish plated with bacteria. We then placed a quarter in the centers of the plated dishes and put them all in the incubator. Two days later, the dishes were covered with a sheet of bacteria—except for a clear ring surrounding each quarter.

"It's the silver in that quarter," the teacher explained. "Bacteria do not like metal ions and enough of the silver leaches out into the media to kill them."

Hurray for George Washington, I thought. I really ought to tell Mom. She'll say it isn't true. Of course, that was the point of the experiment. Everyone's mother held the same opinion. Money was filthy—literally.

But after thinking about the experiment some more, I realized telling Mom would end in an argument. Maybe my knowing the truth was enough.

Arguments about religious issues were common. The Sabbath restrictions, kosher foods, and biblical inter-pretations were endless sources of conflicts. "All those Saturday restrictions don't make any sense," I would say, "Especially living in a society where all kinds of things happen on Saturday."

"The Bible says it is the day of rest and that's good enough for me," she would answer.

"Then why can't it be Sunday like it is for everybody else?" I would ask.

Mom would put her hands on her hips and sigh, "Because we are not Christians. We are Jews and Saturday is our day of rest."

The kosher business was just as big an annoyance. It all began years earlier with my never being able to eat the school lunches. My Boy Scout career was aborted when I wasn't allowed to go on camping trips because the food wouldn't be kosher.

"Kosher made some sense back in biblical times," I declared. "It was the basis of the public health laws. Nobody knew about the germ theory or trichinosis. Who cares if a cow chews its cud and pigs don't. And what's the big deal about fish scales. It's all archaic now. Pork is fine if the pigs are grain fed and the meat cooked properly. And taking chickens to that old man with the beard with his sharp knife and him charging us to do what Dad or I could do for free with a hatchet is money wasted."

Then there were the questions about biblical teachings. They troubled me. "How could God make a woman from a man's rib? Why would God even suggest Abraham sacrifice his son, Isaac, and how about killing those innocent Egyptian first-born sons even if their fathers were bad guys? Do two wrongs make a right?

"Don't you think Jacob deceiving poor old Isaac to get his blessing instead of his good brother Esau was kind of underhanded? Don't you think God might have disapproved?"

And, my final shot was often, "The parting of the Red Sea so Moses could lead the Children out of slavery is impossible. It has got to be a fairy tale."

Mom would patiently explain to me that the laws governing all the rituals were written in the Talmud by very wise men and were, therefore, inviolate. I think she knew that my questions were more than just a search for answers but were meant to challenge her unyielding acceptance of the edicts. As the barrage of dissent and defiance kept coming at her she reluctantly relented on some of the issues. Saturday sports and driving the car for school-related activities became acceptable—as long as Dad didn't have to drive me. She had a practical reason, of course. Anything I did that led to success at school was good. She could look away and bend the divine laws in exchange for getting ahead in the world.

Mom's anger directed toward Nazi Germany led to more heated discussions. "The holocaust is a sin against humanity, she'd say."

So I'd ask, "How could God allow the Holocaust to occur—and how about the Crusades and the Spanish inquisition?" She had no answers for me, she would just shake her head.

Reason never prevailed. And there was no enlisting Dad's help. He had bought into it. All he would ever say was, "It is useless to argue with your mother and I wish you'd finally figure that out for yourself."

Still, I'd won the practical argument over playing sports and driving on Saturday. They were most important, but that didn't stop me from pursuing the others.

"Sometimes I think you just want to argue," Mom would often say to me.

There was some truth in her observation but it was more than that. I had accepted the wisdom of Micah, "And what does the Lord require of you? To act justly and to love mercy and to walk humbly with your God." That made sense to me. And I liked the Bible stories, full of daring adventures and miracles. My problem was Mom's literal acceptance and following all the rituals. The devilish details—abstract theological philosophy converted to bare everyday reality—was the grist for our battleground.

THE PERFECT SUMMER

THE FEED ROOM of the brooder house was covered with a fine layer of chicken mash, like powdered sugar on one of Mom's cakes. I had cleaned out the small amount of grain and mash that remained in the bins that lined the wall of the room. The left-over feed filled several buckets that now stood neatly near the door to the outside.

It was May and the brooder house was empty. We'd finished transferring the pullets to the range for their summer vacation. Mine was also approaching. As I put the finishing touches on cleaning the feed room, sweeping the mash-covered floor, I watched Dad walk toward me through the haze of swirling mash dust that I was stirring up. He wasn't carrying any tools or egg baskets as he usually did. His resolute walk could only mean he was looking for me. This was not a good sign.

"We need to have a talk," he began. He looked down at the floor. I put the broom handle under my arm and, pushing a net of cobwebs aside, leaned against the wall. "Your mother and I have decided you have to get a job away from home this summer. We want you to find a place to live—away from here—for a few months. That would be good for all of us."

I knew what it was. Mom and I were constantly

arguing—mostly about the seemingly endless restrictions of Orthodox Judaism and her health-related rituals. We were clashing about the most mundane issues, like the best way to scrape manure off of shoes. Mom had an opinion about everything and I was challenging every one of them. In Mom's words, I was a "rebel" and, I suppose, I was.

"I've asked you over and over again to just be quiet and not fight with her," Dad said with a sigh. He placed his hands on the open feed bin and gazed into it. "That's what I do to keep peace. Your reasoning doesn't make any difference. Her mind is set." He paused, finally turning to me and patting me on the back. "The classified ads are a place to start."

It was a good idea. The summer before had been miserable. I had no friends in the neighborhood and I felt lonely. I read books, practiced the violin, helped Dad on the farm, went to the beach with Mom and Frank, and argued with Mom—argued endlessly with Mom.

The classifieds were no help. None of the jobs allowed me to live away from home. I had heard about other kids working at beach resorts in the summer. I finally drove to Asbury Park and made the rounds of hotels. They all saw me as too young and with no experience. They were mostly looking for waiters, busboys, and bellhops and I had no skill at any of those jobs.

"I'm willing to work hard," I said at each visit. How hard can it be to bus tables or wash dishes, I thought? They would shrug me off.

The Asbury Arms, two blocks from the boardwalk, took me on as an elevator operator. It wasn't what I wanted but it was my only offer. It came with room and board.

Asbury Park was in its hey day and working there was fun. Crowds converged on the boardwalk from the Casino to the Convention Hall, especially on weekend nights.

The whirling Casino merry-go-round horses, lions, unicorns, and dragons, saddled in pink, blue, red, green, and trimmed with gold and fake gems slid up and down on metal posts that skewered them to the carousel. In the nearby lake, young lovers and older couples maneuvered their paddle boats between the disinterested swans. It was a different world and a sharp contrast to the serious business of operating a chicken farm—a world of hard work and responsibility. Asbury Park was a place where people relaxed and laughed and had fun. And it was a world without Mom to opine endlessly about the dangers of everything.

Stalls on the boardwalk hawked miraculous vegetable slicers and small plastic inserts for oranges to create instant juice. Booths sold popcorn, cotton candy, salt water taffy, hot dogs, and hamburgers. Convention Hall featured the big bands—Benny Goodman, Jimmy Dorsey, Guy Lombardo, and the voices of Perry Como, Patti Page, and Nat King Cole filled the warm summer nights.

All the people I worked with were college students. They were all waitresses and bellhops except for Al, my roommate and the only waiter, and me. We lived in musty rooms in the basement of the hotel.

Al was a medical student who was solidly built just like Dad but, in contrast, had the smile and aura of a man full of optimism. He carried the heavy dining room trays of food high above his shoulder, balancing them on the tips of four fingers, as if they were weighed down by only feathers.

"For a smart boy, your use of the English language is not very sophisticated," he said after our first week together. "I haven't heard a single four-syllable word out of you. If you want to get into a good university, you need to fix that."

"How do I do that?" I asked.

"I bought this book for you," he said, as he handed me a paperback book entitled, *Twenty Days to Increase Your Word Power*. Al was my hero. I poured over the book every evening. By the end of the summer, I had memorized it and knew a lot of new big words.

Running the elevator was boring. Once in a while, when the bellhops were busy, I got to carry a suitcase or two. I was proud of the few tips I made and decided I'd be a bellhop next year.

"I've learned one thing this summer," I said to Al. "If you want to make tips, you need to be obsequious and sycophantic."

Al smiled. "Not bad," he said.

The girls that worked with us as waitresses adored Al and treated me like their kid brother. After they served lunch, we'd go to the beach a few blocks away. I'd never been so close to so many pretty girls in bathing suits. I even got a couple of kisses.

The bands at Convention Hall had everyone's attention. The highlight for me was Harry James and his band. They were staying right there, at the Asbury Arms. I couldn't afford the concert at Conventional Hall but an impromptu performance at the hotel was my first big band recital. I stood in the back of the lobby feeling overwhelmed.

I didn't see Mom and Dad or Frank all summer. Dad came by every two weeks to pick up my laundry bag and deliver the fresh clothes Mom had washed, but he came in the afternoon when I was working or at the beach.

Mom and Dad finally did show up to see me. They arrived in a new green Chevy on a late afternoon day in August and parked in front of the hotel. As I came back from the beach with Al I almost walked past them not realizing who they were.

"I can't believe you bought a new car," I said.

"What happened to our blue Chevy?"

"It's at home," Dad answered. "We thought you could use it. I won't have to drive you around anymore."

Wow, I thought, my own car. It was almost a perfect summer. All I needed was a girlfriend to start the new school year. I was on the lookout from the first day back.

There was no doubt in my mind that Mary was the prettiest girl in the high school. Every lunch hour she sat at the Lost and Found table in front of the principal's office. I walked by her every day during the first two weeks of school. Her posture reminded of my favorite painting by James Whistler. Her finely-sculpted features would, more likely, have been designed by Gustav Klimt. Once she looked at me and smiled.

One of my classmates told me her name. I practiced the different speeches that might be effective in meeting her. In the end, I walked straight up to her and said, "Hi. I'm Lud. Would you like to go to a movie with me?" I held my breath for a moment.

"I'm Mary and I'd like that," she answered. I relaxed and smiled.

We sat in my ten-year-old blue Chevy parked on a quiet tree-lined street near Georgian Court College. I could barely see Mary sitting next to me in the darkness, her hands folded primly in her lap. Only a space of night-time stillness separated us although it seemed a solid barrier to me. It was a chilly night and I moved closer to the warmth of her body. We were talking about the movie we had just seen but my feeling of excitement didn't come from the conversation. The glow of a distant streetlight splashed on her long black hair that seemed to melt into the shadows of the night.

Our conversation about the movie we had just seen was polite. *Kind Hearts and Coronets* was sort of a murder mystery, and we talked about it for an hour in the dark.

We agreed it was unfortunate that Mazzini, the main character, made the fatal mistake of bragging about murdering his relatives and got caught. Such a lot of talk, such serious, formal conversation, but there was more behind the talk, at least on my part. Recollections of the summer and my parents were forgotten. My real thoughts, as I leaned into the driver's seat, were how best to put an arm around Mary's shoulder and kiss her.

Kissing Mary remained my single overriding focus. I felt like the striving Mazzini, and took heart from his dogged resolve and resourcefulness in reaching his goal. My pulse racing and overcome with seventeen-year-old desire, I finally put my arm on her shoulder and moved toward her.

It was still September and fall was not quite here. It had been the perfect summer.

GIRLFRIEND

I LOOKED THROUGH the car window, and then down at my empty hand, in disbelief. The car doors were locked and the key was still in the ignition. I was parked in front of a bar on an isolated stretch of East Main Street, a mile out of Freehold, in the late afternoon. In those days before cell phones, I was going in to call Mary on a pay phone, hoping she had some free time to spend with me. The minute I got out of the car, I realized what I had done.

Suddenly, the focus of my attention had shifted away from Mary. It was centered on the unreachable key sealed inside the car.

Damn, I thought. I'd done the same thing a few weeks earlier when a school friend and I had wandered the deserted beach in Asbury Park. When we got back, I discovered I had locked the keys in the car. We solved the problem by breaking a small side window with a rock.

"You did what?" Dad yelled at me. "This is an unneeded expense. George Matthews doesn't fix windows for free. You should have called me and I'd have come with another key.

"And don't let there be a next time," he had added, but here it was and here I was. For a moment, I thought of breaking that same window but that idea was out. The

obvious and only solution was to call home and have Dad
bring the spare key. Looking at the bar, I guessed Dad
would be displeased by where I was as much as by my
bothering him. The graying building was old and dilapidated. The roof sagged and some of the shingles were
missing. The homemade sign advertising beer was faded
by years of sun, rain, and cold and needed painting. The
only sign of life was a black Ford pickup parked next to
my car.

Inside, two older men talked with the bartender about
sports, their glasses of beer sitting idly in front of them.
No one turned to look at me. The grimy pay phone was
near the door. I called Dad—he said he'd be there in
fifteen minutes. He didn't sound pleased to be called from
his chores.

Back outside, I leaned against the side of the Chevy,
glancing over my shoulder at the unreachable key firmly
fixed in the ignition. I checked the door handle—it was
still locked. I kicked the front tire and leaned back against
the door. I dreaded my father's wrath.

"I can't believe you were at that bar," he said when he
saw me. "What in the world was going through your
mind when you stopped here?"

He ignored my, "I was looking for a telephone,"
excuse.

"Were you trying to pick up a woman?" He was angri-
er with me than I could remember. He gestured toward
the bar, "The only women you meet in a place like this are
prostitutes."

Discussing anything about sex with Dad was even less
likely than talking about his World War I experiences.
Those conversations were always with Mom. But
prostitutes? We'd never talked about that. What was Dad
thinking about?

I wanted to ask Dad if he knew any prostitutes or if

he'd ever met one. I'd read Somerset Maugham's story about Sadie Thompson, who seduced a self-righteous missionary, and that was the extent of my knowledge. As it happened I'd read the story during the week Dad's Dresden secretary, now living in New York City, visited us on the farm. Her tight dresses emphasized her extra rolls of flesh. I had to consciously avoid looking at her ample breasts that seemed ready to pop out of her outfit. Combined with her cherry-red lips, she was my fantasy of a prostitute.

I was glad when Dad drove her to Pine View on Highway 9 to catch the bus to the city. Mom seemed pleased to see her go, too.

"It's taking your father a long time to get back," she said. "The bus must be running late."

Maybe he'd left early so he could park and kiss her, I thought. When he got back I checked his face for any tell-tale lipstick. I was relieved not to see any and, at the same time, I felt embarrassed, my imaginings about my Dad and the woman had gone beyond kisses.

After Dad unlocked the car, I followed him home. When I got out of the car I said, "I'm sorry about making you come after me. I really was just looking for a phone to talk with a friend."

What I didn't say was that I had planned on calling Mary. I couldn't call from home since I might be over-heard. Mom would disapprove.

"Well, at least you didn't break a window to get the key," Dad said. His anger had been, as always, short-lived. He walked silently into the house ahead of me. I knew there was more to come.

After dinner, Mom turned to me and asked flatly, "Are you still dating that girl?"

I didn't answer. Is this just coincidence, I wondered, or did she just guess I was trying to call Mary?

"I suppose that means yes," she said. "I don't understand why you can't date Jewish girls."

"You want me to date some of those girls who run around with Abe Garfinkle?" I asked, with what I thought was a superior expression.

"You're trying to start an argument," she said, shaking a wooden spoon at me. "There are lots of nice Jewish girls. You don't need to go after the Christians."

"Mom, I like Mary. She's my friend. There's nothing wrong with that."

"Do her parents know she's going out with a Jewish boy?" she asked.

"I don't know."

Actually, I was pretty sure they did. Mary told me her father had talked to Mr. Megill at the hardware store. He told her dad that we were a fine family, she had said. I was sure our being Jewish had come up. I didn't want to talk about it anymore but Mom was persistent.

"No good can come of this," Mom continued. "The Christians tolerate us but then they find some excuse to start a pogrom. We learned our lesson. You always have to be ready to move on and if you have a Christian wife she won't want to go with you. That's what happened to friends in Germany and they died in the concentration camps."

"Mom, I'm not getting married," I was getting whiney and I knew it, "I'm just going out with a friend." I said it slowly, hoping to cut off the conversation.

"I'll tell you how important it is," Mom wasn't listening. "I had an aunt who married a Christian. Just before my grandmother died she said the aunt could not be part of the funeral procession. That meant the aunt had to walk alone one hundred meters behind. Can you imagine that, one hundred meters behind?"

"I can't believe that," I said. "That is so mean."

"It's not mean at all, it shows how important religion is and why you stick to your own," she said. "You get punished if you don't."

"I think you had a cruel grandmother. She's like one of the Grimms' wicked witches."

We were going over the same old ground. Mom hated the Christian Germans, she was never going to set foot on German soil again—and she distrusted Christians even though most of her closest friends were not Jewish.

"Look, Mom," I said. "This isn't Germany—this is the United States. The Bill of Rights says we have freedom of religion. Jews are not persecuted here and I don't need to go any place and anyway, I'm not getting married."

"The Bill of Rights?" she scowled. "It's just a piece of paper. The politicians can change it any time they want to. That's what happened in Germany. We thought we were Germans. Then Hitler came along and said we weren't."

"Mom, this country is different. We had a civil war to bring the Negroes out of slavery. And we did fight against the Nazis, you remember, it was called World War II."

"All I know is, you have to be prepared," she said. "That's why you should be a musician or a scientist or a doctor. They can't take your knowledge and skills away from you but they can take everything else." There was no winning against Mom, but at least she was on another tack—one that was more constructive than criticizing my choice of a girlfriend.

PRINCETON

AS I THINK ABOUT MY PARENTS from the vantage point of age and distance, I realize I am a combination of them both. Mom always kept swimming as the mouse did in her favorite story until it had churned the milk into firm butter, climbed out on top, and run away to freedom. "If you work hard enough," she often told me, "anything is possible."

Dad saw only the hard work.

Mom was the ultimate survivor and she instilled that trait in me. She had survived her mother's suicide when only a small child, and then weathered growing up in an orphanage. She endured the dread of German Nazism and worked with Dad to arrange our escape to America. She watched the inexorable defeat of Hitler and his German army but VE Day came too late for relatives and friends who couldn't or wouldn't or didn't dare to get out in time. Hitler's defeat, however, fulfilled another of her German sayings—powerful despots don't reign long. This one lasted long enough, however, to color her convictions for the rest of her life. She never trusted governments and watched for the time we would again be on the run. Still, she took great joy in music and family and especially in Frank's and my successes.

My Dad was full of angst and sadness, especially at home. Being a soldier in the First World War had left its scars on his soul and he was demoralized by the loss of his successful business career, the result of the second war. He spent long hours working alone, I'm sure by choice. What he thought about at these lonely times we never knew.

Dad was a different person in public. When he was out shopping or dealing with customers, he was warm and gregarious. As his English improved, he became even more outgoing and I could see how he was a star in business in Germany, before the war.

For two decades, he and Mom struggled to establish their farm as a successful enterprise, to educate Frank and me, and to restore the family's good fortunes. Because of their determination—working every day with no let-up—they were successful and the farm and family prospered.

Being driven out of Germany with her family convinced Rosi that we were part of the Diaspora that was cursed to wander from one nation to another. She wanted her boys to be prepared for the inevitable. A portable profession was, in her mind, of critical importance.

During the early years, my mom did a great deal of pushing and shoving to get me to participate in her ambitious agenda. A third grade report card spoke of my, "dreaming, talking, and wasting his time," much to my mother's chagrin and consternation. My occasional disciplinary visits to the principal's office were usually met with displeasure and disapproval at home. During later years I became a much more willing participant.

Mom had considerable help in her efforts. Our two music teachers and the public librarian were her close confidantes and allies. They urged her on whenever she doubted us, usually after an argument or a note from school made her despair.

Now, as a high school senior, the moment of truth had arrived for me. It was time to apply to colleges. I listened carefully to my advisor. "You've done well in school," he said, "and you should have an excellent chance of being accepted by our state university, Rutgers. They've taken a number of our graduates in recent years. There are other good universities, too, like Susquehanna and Penn State, but I really think you need to focus on Rutgers."

"What about Princeton or one of the other Ivy League schools?" I asked.

"Those are beyond the horizon of our students," he answered, taking off his glasses and not looking at me. "I wouldn't waste my time on those applications." I knew that wouldn't go over with Mom at all.

For her, Princeton was a special place. She knew that Rutgers was a fine university and did not share the recent history of anti-Semitism with Princeton. Still, Princeton was one of the premier American universities. Mom was aware of the university's reputation before the need for our family to immigrate to the United States became a necessity. Princeton was Albert Einstein's university and that helped assuage her bigotry concerns. And, like Rutgers, it was nearby. Princeton had always been her dream for my brother and me and that, was that.

The trouble was that no one from our small-town high school had ever gone to Princeton. Lillian Wilbur, the principal, made that abundantly clear to me when I delivered the application to her office for her endorsement.

"Who put you up to this idea?" Mrs. Wilbur asked, her large body firmly planted in the black padded armchair behind her desk. Her back was impossibly straight and rigid, as if she had been born to the role of judge. She was always intimidating and her posture was meant to show her unbending nature. She understood order and expected everyone and everything to be in their proper places.

Of course, so did Mom.

"My Mom thinks it's the place to go," I answered.

The slightest smile spread across her thin lips. She looked at me over her glasses. "I'll give her a call. You need to look at some more reasonable choices."

I knew she liked my parents. Dad delivered eggs to their house every Thursday for years and he made sure they were extra big double-yolkers. Mom and Dad spoke about her with the greatest admiration. She was a respected woman in Freehold and Dad viewed delivering eggs to her as an honor and a privilege.

To me, Mrs. Wilbur was a force with which I had to reckon. But then, so was Mom. It'll be interesting to see how this plays out, I thought.

Mom didn't listen to Mrs. Wilbur's discouraging observations about Princeton. The pronouncement fell on deaf ears. Dad might have succumbed to Mrs. Wilbur's negative assessment but Mom was after the pot at the rainbow's end. Princeton was still the goal. And by now it had also become my goal. Princeton would mean that we had really arrived. Going to Princeton was the pinnacle of success for Mom and it had become so for me.

I spent an entire Sunday evening filling out the two applications—one for admission and the other for a scholarship. There was a section for Dad to complete—stating his annual income and the sum he would contribute yearly to my education.

"You make only $3,000 a year," I asked in amazement, "and you're going to contribute $1,000 to my tuition? How can you do that? That's a third of your income."

He had put down the *Aufbau* and gone into the dining room where he stored all his financial records. Now he looked up from the application form and pushed last year's tax form aside. "It is a lot of money but the percentage is deceiving," he began.

Mom must have known what was coming. She turned from the dinner dishes she was washing in the sink, looking sternly at us.

"The boy doesn't need to know what you want to tell him," she said.

"He's old enough that he needs to begin understanding about the world of finance," he replied.

He explained to me that the annual income derived from the income tax form was after all the farm expenses had been deducted. Repairs, electricity, telephone, car expenses, everything except food, clothes, and going to the movies, had been subtracted.

"That's how you figure income," he finished.

I remained impressed by the amount he was contributing to my education. "It's still a lot of money," I said.

Mom turned back to her dishes. The smile on her face said she was satisfied with the outcome of our talk.

Late one spring afternoon, when I was coming home from track practice I saw my parents through the window sitting quietly at the kitchen table. This was usually a busy time of the day for them and I knew from past experience, that this was a bad omen. It probably meant I was in big trouble although I didn't have a clue as to what I had done wrong this time.

When I entered the kitchen, I was surprised that neither one launched into a discussion of my latest transgression. Instead, they were looking at two envelopes lying in the middle of the table. They would never have opened them since they were addressed to me. Later I realized that my parents had sat there much of the afternoon wondering about the contents.

The larger of the two envelopes looked formal. It had the orange and black seal of Princeton University embossed adjacent to the return address. The address on the smaller one had obviously been typed with an old portable typewriter—the letters somewhat askew. Like my parents, I realized the big moment had arrived.

The only sound in the kitchen was the soft hum of the refrigerator standing in the corner. There was none of the usual animated conversation that always filled the room. I opened the smaller envelope and read it silently.

"I'm getting a scholarship to Princeton." I announced, grinning. "If I do well, I'll keep it for four years."

The second envelope was the formal acceptance.

Tears welled up in Dad's eyes and began streaming down his face. Mom beamed. They both got up and Mom hugged me. Dad walked around the table to shake my hand. The years of hard work, struggle, and pushing and shoving had paid off. Their dream was beginning to come true.

I walked into homeroom a few mornings later. The usual excited early morning discussions of yesterday's events came to an abrupt stop—the room suddenly went quiet. All eyes were on me. Was my shirt buttoned wrong? Were my pants unzipped? No, that wasn't it. One of the girls held up the front page of the sports section of the Freehold Transcript, our weekly paper that came out every Thursday. "Gutmann Gets Scholarship," the headline declared, and right below was a picture of me on the track at the start of a race. My classmates seemed in awe. I was pleased but also a little embarrassed. Still, this was the big moment—the realization of my fantasy of the last four years. No one else would match that sports headline. I had arrived.

When I got home that night from practice Mom had her own thoughts about the headline, the picture, and the article. "The paper always gets it wrong," she said. "I know you're good at track but we all know you got an academic scholarship. Putting it in the sports section says it was because of your running. Your Dad's calling the paper tomorrow and have them clarify it next week."

She was going to ruin everything. "Wait a minute," I replied. "You know why I got that scholarship but if all my friends want to think it was for sports that's not so bad either. Please do me a big favor and forget it."

She took a good long look at me. I thought she was trying really hard not to smile. That was the end of it.

The trip to Princeton was forty miles—it took about one hour. Hard to believe, but we hadn't seen the university before the acceptance. My interview had been with a local attorney that no one seemed to know and forty miles was farther in the days when speed limits were forty-five miles an hour and all roads were local. Mom and Dad were silent during the trip, each engrossed in their private thoughts. The journey from Dresden to Princeton had been long and tortuous, full of impediments and obstructions. They had survived the harrowing events of the 1930s and fourteen years of long hours of work, anxiety, and fitting into a new society. One of their children at Princeton was success for all. We would now see the campus together for the first time.

We drove through the farming countryside of open pastures, cornfields, barns, chickenhouses and gas stations. The elmtree-lined street leading into the historic town blended in with the rest of the bucolic setting we had driven through.

My reverie came to an abrupt end. "I can't believe it," I exclaimed, "look at that spire towering over the trees."

A few minutes later the pastoral country scenes were transformed into a succession of Gothic and Romanesque buildings, transporting us into a different world. Dad drove silently up Washington Road and then onto Nassau Street, the gateway to the storied university. Mom broke the silence. "It reminds me of Heidelberg but without the castle," she said. Tears welled up in Dad's eyes.

We stopped the car in front of Nassau Hall and admired the two-century-old building. I read from a brochure about the university, "It was the capital of our country for a while in the beginning," I said. "In 1783, the Continental Congress met here for six months. Our country was coming out of the Revolutionary War, a conflict fought by immigrants to free themselves from religious and political persecution."

Mom leaned into the back seat of the car, her arms folded across her chest. "No," she said, "it's better than Heidelberg. And Nassau Hall is more impressive than the castle."

Dad's cheeks glistened as he blew his nose. His voice broke as he said, "This is a wonderful place in a wonderful country. They say here anything is possible, and they are right."

REGENSBURG TO LANGROCK'S

OUR RED FORD pickup truck, dulled and tarnished from years of heat, rain, and cold, stood in the shade of the chickenhouse feed room. It sagged under the weight of the hundred-pound sacks of grain I was piling one by one in its bed. It was a chore I'd done so many times that my mind was elsewhere, thinking about my summer job at a nearby restaurant that would begin in a few weeks, calculating the amount of tip money I was likely to earn to go with the scholarships I had for medical school in the fall, and wondering if it would be enough. The last final exams at Princeton had been three days before and graduation was still two weeks away. Helping out on the farm was an expected time-filler and it gave me the mental leisure to ruminate and remember.

Princeton had been a bitter-sweet experience. Intense studying, especially in my early years, led to loneliness, despite many friends. I had spent hours working in my room, a flickering fluorescent light illuminating my desk, or studying alone on weekends in the dark recesses of the impressive Firestone Library—reading, writing, memorizing; absorbing. The movie image of a group of college students cramming for an exam, now and then bursting into a song, and then returning to work together has always been far from the truth. Saturday's high point was often going alone or with a few friends to the late movie. By senior year I'd traded the library for my thesis advisor's research lab, and, although I often worked alone there, too, it was with the excitement of finding new insights into my thesis subject.

I had finished my assigned task and loaded all the bags of feed into the truck. The current farm dog came along wagging her tail and stopped for a pat. I began to mentally drift back into earlier years, remembering days on the farm and back to grammar school.

Thinking back, I realized my childhood was also often a lonely time, living out in the country with few neighbors and no friends except those in school. That changed in high school, especially once I got my driver's license. When you're a farm boy, life really begins with getting that all-important license. You feel like you've grown up overnight. No more school bus, no more looking for a lift or hitching a ride—and after I got a car in my senior year, I could practice for track meets or hang out with friends or take my girlfriend out whenever I liked. After graduation, I was ready to move on to university life.

I thought I'd finally left the religious prejudice of grade school behind when I entered high school but that was merely a lull. Princeton University had discontinued its quotas on Jewish student enrollment but the Princeton eating clubs firmly kept their distance; they were the university's answer to traditional college fraternities.

All junior and senior students had to join one; there was nowhere else to eat during the last two years. The selection process of new members—interviewing the sophomore students in their rooms during appointed evening hours—was managed by senior students who embodied all the evils of exclusive country club bigotry.

Most clubs had Jewish quotas. I joined Prospect Club, one that did not make being a Christian an asset. The lone African-American student, who became a good friend, couldn't afford the cost of a club at all but was fed sub rosa by the kind ladies who worked in the student infirmary.

The main reason, however, that I joined Prospect was its being the only cooperative club. While the other clubs had numerous employees, Prospect had only two cooks. That meant the annual cost was much lower than at the other clubs. There were no waiters and houseboys to employ—we did all the work ourselves and this well suited my limited budget. It got even better my senior year when I served as the club steward. I made the weekly menus and organized the kitchen activities for which I got free room and board.

Still, the club selection experience—the well-named, "bicker"—left me with a cynical view of the social milieu of the university. Anti-Semitism was strangely accepted in higher education just as it had been in public school, even with the horrors of the Nazi camps so recently revealed.

"Bicker is a social system run by a bunch of guys barely out of their teens," my roommate observed. "It's bound to be a catastrophe."

"It's like *Lord of the Flies*," I said. It was William Golding's newly-published book about a group of schoolboys who survive a plane crash and try to govern themselves. Their descent into savage behavior had disastrous results.

"It sure is," my friend said. "The only difference is that instead of killing one another, bicker just ostracizes."

As I threw the last sack on the truck, my reverie was interrupted by Mom walking briskly down the rough gravel path toward me. Her determined look predicted a plan for this warm spring morning. It would probably be good—certainly better than what I was doing. I was bored and I knew that next task, sweeping the feed room, would be no better.

Mom always got right into it. "I think you need a new suit for your college graduation. How about we drive over to Princeton and buy one?" she announced, looking up at me, her hands firmly planted on her hips. It wasn't really a question.

"I'll talk to your father," she said, giving my cheek an affectionate pat and turning away immediately. It seemed like a good idea to me.

As I watched her walk off, purposeful as always, I thought how deeply my relationship with her had changed over the past four years. She no longer tried to impose any of her rules and rituals on me and accepted my independence and my move away from following the tenets of Orthodox Judaism.

I suppose my rejection of her religious views was inevitable. I had decided they were not based on any inherent intellectual conviction on her part, but rather reflected her deep-seated anger toward Germany. She knew I refused to be included in her flat promise to God that if He would save her family, she would observe His laws to the letter—and so would we. Leave it to Mom to set up the terms of a bargain with God. It was not a Faustian bargain, however, she did it for us even though we (Frank and me, that is; how Dad felt we never knew) didn't appreciate it. Mom had a personality that lent itself to ritual and the complex patterns and proscriptions of the faith were perfect for her. When I left the house for the university, she accepted my new life.

I remember her announcing more than once at dinner, "So what happened to Lud at Princeton? He came under the spell of Professor Walter Kaufman, the great Nietzsche expert. I've had my fill of the Nietzsche philosophy—that there couldn't be a God with all the evil in this world, and, if there is, he must be a malevolent and mischievous God.

"I'll tell you who is mischievous. It's Walter Kaufman, that's who—taking young boys and filling their heads with nonsense." For her, Kaufman was the great infidel.

"Mom," I had told her, "you would have approved of some of Nietzsche's beliefs."

"Never," she said.

"He didn't like Richard Wagner and disapproved of German anti-Semitism," I answered. I knew that would stop her. It did for a moment.

"You know how to make a good argument," she said.

"I'm not against Judaism," I replied, "not at all. I agree with you that it has a lot to teach us. It's just that the reformed Judaism is much more to my liking than orthodox."

For me, Micah had summed it all up with his famous "to act justly and to love mercy and to walk humbly with your God." It wasn't what she wanted but I think she thought it was a reasonable compromise.

In the end, however, her view of Princeton never wavered. It was still the great university and Walter Kaufman. . . well, she just finally let him slip into the background. She was proud that Frank would be a Princeton freshman in the fall.

Dad was coming from the nearby chickenhouse carrying two wire buckets filled with freshly-laid eggs. Mom headed toward him. "Lud needs a suit for graduation," she announced. "I want to go to Princeton to buy it."

Dad put the two buckets down. "I have so much work to do," he answered. "Can't we get it in Lakewood or Asbury Park? A trip to either one would take less time and be less expensive."

"No, I'm sure it needs to be that Ivy League style," she said. "It'll be much easier to find it in Princeton."

Yes, I thought, she has the style business right. We need to go to Princeton.

"OK," Dad sighed. "I'll have to get cleaned up. I guess we're going now."

Mom nodded.

Even though he complained, I knew Dad would like a break and, besides, he always enjoyed shopping. I could have made the trip alone with Mom. It was unusual that she seemed to want his support for this one.

Dad handed me the keys. "Pull the car out while I change my clothes," he said.

Twenty minutes later the three of us were on our way on the short drive through the New Jersey countryside. Unlike our first trip to Princeton, this time I drove the car with Dad sitting next to me.

Driving to Princeton was no longer an awe-inspiring event. True, the Gothic towers and peaked roofs rising above the trees still seemed out of place in the midst of the New Jersey farmlands, but they had lost their mystique for me after four years. The imposing stone walls felt like home.

As we drove along, I sat back and my musings began again. Princeton had changed my whole view of the world. It all began the first week of my English literature course.

The professor teaching us shook his head, "You guys are taking this Shakespeare too seriously," he said. "Read that last speech of Mercutio's again—out loud, Bill, and with some feeling, if you can."

In my first week at Princeton, I was struggling with freshman English. We were all struggling with freshman English. A classmate read the passage from *Romeo and Juliet* again in halting phrases.

"'This cannot anger him: 'twould anger him
To raise a spirit in his mistress' circle
Of some strange nature, letting it there stand
Till she had laid it and conjured it down;'"
We all watched our professor intently. There must
be something important in the passage but no one seemed
to get it. We were trying too hard to get the deeply philo-
sophical meaning we were sure must be just beyond us.

"Come on fellows," he intoned, and not without
sarcasm, "This is not some sanitized, high school version
of Shakespeare. This is the real stuff."

A pause. Twelve young men looking serious. He
sighed and read it again slowly "Listen carefully, 'raising
a spirit in his mistress' circle'—use your imagination,
gentlemen—'letting it there stand until she has laid it...'
Do I need to draw a picture for you guys?"

The laughter was sudden and explosive. It was clear,
and we got it. The professor looked satisfied. He closed
the book.

This was the first of many lessons—the hormones
were overflowing in Mercutio and Romeo just as they
were in my eleven classmates and me. Surprises, insights,
awakenings pervaded nearly every class.

Walter Kaufman overwhelmed us with his Philosophy
of Religion course. "Buzzer" Hall made European history
come alive and stirred us with adventurous exploits of
Giuseppe Garibaldi in unifying Italy. John Turkevich
taught and demonstrated chemistry—in between colorful
chemical reactions and anticipated explosions. It was
like the Fourth of July fireworks all year long. Colin
Pittendrigh introduced us to biological time clocks and
how the circadian rhythms of midges made it possible for
them to spawn in the ocean tidal zones. A demonstration
of sensible natural science, at work in every animal
including young Princeton students—like the midges,

ready to obey natural laws.

So here I was, at this spectacular sanctuary of learning, suddenly immersed in all the great disciplines and more. It was an immersion in other ways, too. Princeton was only forty miles down the road from our chicken farm outside of Freehold and our country high school, but I felt I was on a different planet. And indeed, I was. The farms and small towns of New Jersey had not prepared me for the intellectual challenges, the stunning old-world architecture and the students who were unique to Princeton.

The campus of my four years was teeming with young men wearing khakis, white tee shirts, and stylishly-dirty white buckskin shoes. Most seemed to have gone to prep schools and I thought they were better prepared for the intense educational process we were going through. I quickly learned that my ability to write was woefully deficient and almost failed my freshman English writing course. Still, armed with a generous scholarship and a part-time job at the Campus Center Snack Bar, I was going to soak up all the knowledge I could on my way to medicine. At Princeton, you got (you were awarded, to say it properly), a BA—an arts degree. A science degree was not offered, so I couldn't hide behind my ability in science and math to push up my average.

Goethe referred to the college years as the *Sturm und Drang Jahre*—the years of turmoil and stress, the years of boys growing up to be men. That's what Princeton was all about. For young men (and that's who were there in the 1950s, young men—there were no women) Princeton was a man's intellectual paradise. We were led, cajoled, persuaded, and inspired by an enthusiastic faculty. At least, that's how I remember it.

My required senior thesis had been a great success and I was about to publish a portion of it as my first scientific paper. Aurin Chase, my kindly senior thesis advisor, spent hours with me reviewing my progress.

"When you apply to medical school," he told me, "remember, Columbia and Penn will do their interviews here."

My first interview was with Columbia's Dean of Students. We sat in Dr. Chase's office and talked mostly about my project. Afterwards, I went next door to the lab to work.

I didn't notice Dr. Chase come in until I felt his hand on my shoulder. "The Dean liked you," he said. "He's going to accept you. It'd be a good place to go."

There had been a lot of talk about the complicated application process. It turned out to be easy. I knew Mom and Dad would be pleased since it was prestigious and, besides, the medical school was only three blocks from Uncle Friedl's apartment in New York. I cancelled the Penn interview the next day.

Once classes were finished in May, Princeton, like all college towns, turns back from an active, student-packed community into a sleepy little village populated only with permanent residents. The traffic jams on Nassau Street, students filling the sidewalks as they shop at the men's stores or have a snack at the Balt, and families peering at the Firestone Library, the new gothic chapel, and historic Nassau Hall were momentarily scenes of the past. The usually busy campus was deserted. An occasional unseen power mower broke the silence like a distant thunderstorm breaking the stillness of a quiet spring morning. Overtime workers were getting the campus dressed for the upcoming graduation and alumni reunion.

"Where do you want to go?" I asked my mother. No sense in asking Dad, he always stepped back in these situations and let others decide.

"I suppose Langrock's. They're the best shop?" my mother asked.

"They're fancy and expensive," I replied, smiling.

Mom was frugal—most of the time—but when making important purchases, she always went for the best.

"That's where we're going," she said. This was one of those occasions.

I parked our aging green Chevy sedan in front of Langrock's. The large clothing store display window was ascetically trimmed in white and, in contrast to the fussily over-filled shop exhibits nearby, held only three suits. The headless mannequins all wore Princeton cravats around their necks and their suits were the accepted classic styles, expensively cut from expensive fabrics and, I was sure, sporting expensive price tags. There was only one other car parked on the street. An elderly couple out for their late morning walk smiled at us as we walked toward them.

I'd been to Langrock's before with a few of my friends but had never bought anything. Like the many of the new breed of scholarship students with little disposable cash, I'd found more inexpensive outlets for my clothing needs. Fortunately for us, chino pants, white T-shirts, and scuffed white buckskin shoes (the scuffed effect was important) were the accepted student outfits.

On this quiet weekday morning, Langrock's was uninhabited except for more headless mannequins standing at attention along two walls wearing summer suits; wooden racks with neatly-hung suits and jackets; and two live salesmen, almost hidden by the counters that were covered with an assortment of dress shirts, rep ties and lightweight sweaters. The salesmen were lounging over coffee in the back of the shop and glanced at us without interest. We were the only customers in the store. One of the salesmen ignored us and continued to read his magazine. The other walked over slowly, making a careful appraisal of the three of us. I had seen him before and knew he had spent years catering to the university's wealthy and privileged students. Like the other salesmen in Nassau Street's exclusive shops, they mirrored the elitist and superior attitudes of their clientele.

We didn't measure up at all. There was my dad, still in his unpressed work pants and shoes. He wore one of his old blue silk shirts, its detachable collar long gone, that had seen better days in Germany. It still had smudges on the sleeves from painting the chicken-houses earlier in the spring. His leather shoes, originally fine quality, were in worse shape than the shirt.

Mom wore a simple, patterned housedress, bought in Woolworth's, which had survived a multitude of wash-ings. Her hair was its usual untamed bramble of curls. I was the most fashionable or, at least, acceptable in my white T-shirt and khaki shorts.

The salesman's assessment was less than favorable. He wore the same superior and imperious look so carefully cultivated by some of my more class-conscious school-mates. Mom, busy looking at the racks of suits, paid no attention to him. Dad watched, amused, and soon found a chair the better to observe at a distance. He opened his newspaper to the editorial page.

"I suppose you're just looking?" The salesman said, putting emphasis on the "just." He clearly wanted to get back to his coffee. He had no polite, "Welcome to Langrock's," for us and no obsequious, "What can I do for you today, madam?" for my mother. His carefully-creased gray wool trousers, white shirt and orange and black striped tie enhanced his self-ordained aura of disdain. His nose lifted a notch higher as he watched my mother run her hands across the suits, feeling the goods for qual-ity. I imagined him thinking, what could she possibly know of quality?

In his eyes, we were farmers. He was only interested in

important customers—ones who could pay full freight. The usual friendly comments made to clinch and perhaps expand the sale, such as: "Free alterations? Of course, Madam," or, "Those socks would go well with that suit, sir." or, "Permit me to suggest a tie…" No such thoughts crossed this salesman's mind as he studied us and wished us gone. My father sat in his chair, secretly amused but giving no sign.

"Actually, we want to buy our son a suit. He doesn't have one," Mom finally said in her heavy German accent. I thought I heard the salesman let out a small groan.

"I guess you folks are farmers," he replied, his tone exasperated. "You probably don't get into town too often. Are you really sure this is where you want to buy a suit?"

There, he had said it. Farmers. That's us to him, I thought, just farmers who had wandered in.

"Oh yes, a suit for my son," she replied, her smile radiating her European charm, "he says this is the place to come," gesturing at me.

The salesman looked me over and shrugged. He went over to the rack to pick out several suits. "Our suits are quite expensive." He was really trying to be rid of us.

Mom ignored the remark. "The suit has to be ready in a week since our son graduates from the university here in two weeks. I assume alterations are free?"

The salesman stopped, momentarily caught off guard. Mom kept right on with her assault, "Our younger son will be a freshman here this fall." My father looked over the top of his newspaper.

The salesman was now in full retreat.

"Can you show us something in charcoal gray?" she asked, smiling broadly.

"Yes, madam," he said rather breathlessly, "Will madam wish to select shoes for the graduate? We will be pleased to fit her other son, as well." His large smile glowed with false sincerity.

I didn't dare look at my father. I was sure he had low-ered his newspaper to his lap and taken off his glasses. I could picture his expression. The old salesman in him must have thought, "I bet this young chump can't even tie his own shoes."

How many years had it been? Twenty years since Dad and Uncle Ernst sat at dinner in Regensburg, Germany discussing their fears for their families under Nazi rule. Could they leave, and give up all they had? Eighteen years since my mother and father fled with me and my lit-tle brother, Frank, some furniture and clothes, to safety in America. Sixteen years since Mom and Dad paid the last bit of money they had to buy a farm in New Jersey. And now after those long years of backbreaking work and a frugal country life for my parents, the deserved pleasure in 1955 of a gift for their graduate from Langrock's in Princeton—a gift that symbolized how far we had come.

Epilogue

FINDING FANNY

THE FLIGHT TO FRANKFURT should have been routine. Most of my trips to Germany over the years had been uneventful. Board the plane, have a beer with dinner, sleep most of the trip, and head for work with colleagues at the university in Mainz. This summer's trip, as it turned out, was quite different; it was filled with unease and apprehension, just as the very first one had been, years before.

And the purpose of this visit was different, too. At the invitation of the city of Frankfurt, I was going to explore the past—the past of my parents and the relatives who came before them and the influence of National Socialism upon all our lives. I had no memory of living in Germany. I had been too young. My recollections were from the stories I'd heard growing up—unsettling stories.

My first trip to Frankfurt, forty years before, was at the request of a German friend to work together on a research project. During the flight, I was haunted by my childhood memories, all colored by the Nazi Holocaust. My parents, my brother, and I had escaped and so had most of my relatives but not three cousins, their parents, and my father's mother, all of whom died in concentration camps.

The events fueled my mother's ever-present anger toward Germany's Nazi government and the country's people who had allowed the German disaster to happen. She had vowed never to set foot on German soil again and that resolve dominated my thoughts. Sitting on the plane, thirty years ago, I imagined her in the next seat, admonishing me about my decision to go.

This time I was overcome with all the same anxieties even though I had learned that the Germany of today was far more socially responsible than the one my parents knew seventy years before. In preparation for the visit, I had reviewed old family photographs and letters and corresponded with city representatives. I learned from them that my cousins had perished in the Lublin concentration camp and that my grandmother, my dad's mom, had died in a euthanasia killing camp. Trying to sleep, I had visions of storm troopers roaming cobblestone streets and starving camp-incarcerated prisoners. Dominating it all, I sensed Mom's presence nearby, again rebuking my decision to visit Germany.

"Sorry, Mom," I heard myself whisper, "but this time I wish you were here with me."

Mom would have responded with a disapproving scowl. She saw the disappearance of the three girls and their parents as the essence of Nazi cruelty and the murder of my aging grandmother as an atrocity. The picture of the three cousins, prominently displayed in my parent's living room, was meant to be a perpetual memorial to them. For me, they became an everlasting reminder of the evil side of Germany. As I sat on the plane trying to sleep, the picture of the three girls kept flashing before my eyes.

During my stay, I visited Frankfurt's Jewish Museum,

a Jewish-Christian retirement facility, and the restored historic synagogue in Worms. I talked with Jews now living in Frankfurt and learned about the new Russian makeup of German Jewry. I viewed the historic remains of several homes, wells, and ritual baths in the Jewish ghetto, Judenstrasse (now located in the Jewish Museum), and learned about the anti-Semitism that stalked the Jews through many centuries and was part of the infrastructure of the Holocaust. It was all a stark reminder of an unsavory history that my family had managed to survive.

As part of the trip, I had arranged to visit the Jewish cemetery in Babenhausen. That was where my other grandmother, Fanny, was supposed to be buried. Mom was a small girl when Fanny died and it resulted in my mother growing up in an orphanage. Those events had happened long before the Nazi era began. I recall Mom telling me late in her life that her only unfulfilled wish was to visit her mother's gravesite one last time. But, then, she had sworn never to set foot in Germany again. It would remain only a dream.

The Jewish cemetery in Babenhausen was difficult to find. It was barely visible, nestled among nearby homes. The surrounding chain-linked fence and tall grasses served as a curtain to hide the rows of ancient gravestones lined up like old soldiers, standing at attention. Opening the gate, I marveled at the incongruity of the scene—a neatly-preserved Jewish cemetery in the small town of a country with a terrible history of anti-Semitism.

This was the cemetery Mom had wanted to visit for the half century she lived in the United States, but couldn't. Once a year, on the anniversary of her mother's death, she would go to the Jewish cemetery in Lakewood. She would pick a gravesite, seemingly at random, and spend a quiet half-hour cleaning the gravestone and trimming the grass that surrounded it. Dad would wait patiently in the car—respecting her wish to be alone. "Why do you do it?" I would ask. Her answer was always the same, I would know when I grew up.

I wish you were here, Mom, I thought. And suddenly she was standing next to me. She kissed my cheek and squeezed my hand the way she always had. She looked older than I remembered. Her hair was, as usual, a tangle of uncombed curls, now all white, and her wrinkled face still permanently browned from years working in the summer sun.

You've lost weight, I thought. Her black skirt and cream-colored blouse hung loosely on her thin frame. Her favorite silver brooch covered the top button just beneath her chin.

"I came to find your mother's grave," I said. "You're not mad at me for coming?"

"No, no," she answered, "it's a blessing and I did want to see it one last time. I can't believe we are doing it together." She looked up at me, her eyes glistening with a mother's pride, and she squeezed my hand again.

The cemetery went back several centuries with the most recent grave that of a child who died in 1946. Wandering among the headstones, I thought I had found it. The inscription read, "Fanny Kahn" and the monument had been erected by her husband, Mayer, and her family.

"That's not it," Mom said. "You see, it says she was born an Oppenheimer. My mother was a Schaumberger."

"Curious," I said, "this Fanny's husband had the same name as Opa. What a coincidence."

I searched further and finally found another Fanny Kahn. This time the stone correctly said she was born a Schaumberger. I knew we had found the right marker. As we approached closer, I could see the tears begin to stream along the wrinkles of Mom's crinkled cheeks.

"I was only four years old when she died," she said.

Then in a soft whisper, like a faint breeze, she added, "You know, she committed suicide."

I nodded my head. She had told me years before. It was a family secret that she shared with her sons. "Your Dad doesn't know," she had said.

"I missed her terribly when I was growing up," she added. "I'm so glad you came here."

Stepping forward, I reached deep in my pocket for the stone I'd picked up outside the cemetery. I placed it gently on Fanny's headstone, knowing Mom would be pleased. I turned to her, smiling, but I was alone again.

"You're right, Mom," I said to no one, in particular, "it's a blessing."

About the Author

Lud Gutmann cares for his patients and teaches medical students and residents at West Virginia University Health Sciences Center, where he holds the Hazel Ruby McQuain Chair of Neurology.

His career in medicine began in 1955 after graduation from Princeton University when he attended medical school in  New York City at Columbia University's College of Physicians and Surgeons. This was followed by a neurology residency at the University of Wisconsin and a fellowship in clinical neurophysiology at the Mayo Clinic.

He helped establish the Neurology Department at West Virginia University and chaired the department for twenty eight years. He has been a director of the American Board of Psychiatry and Neurology and has served on the editorial boards of neurological journals. He received an honorary doctorate degree from the University of Mainz, Mainz, Germany in 1993.

His research has focused on diseases of muscles and nerves and he has published more than 175 articles in peer-reviewed journals. He began writing stories about his patients in 2001. They have been published in magazines and journals. In 2009, he gathered a group of these stories into a book, *The Immobile Man: A Neurologist's Casebook.*

This memoir, *Richard Road: Journey from Evil*, will be followed by another short story collection. Dr. Gutmann lives in Morgantown, West Virginia, with Mary Wallis Gutmann, his devoted wife and editor.